Enter in

TAKING POSSESSION OF GOD'S PLAN

DEBORAH RAE STRICKLIN

Enter In: Taking Possession of God's Plan
by Deborah Rae Stricklin

Trade paperback ISBN: 978-1-943294-45-9
Ebook ISBN: 978-1-943294-46-6

Cover design by Martijn van Tilborgh

Published by Dream Releaser Publishing

Enter In is also available on Amazon Kindle, Barnes & Noble Nook and Apple iBooks.

Contents

Foreword

AS YOU READ THE pages of this outstanding book, *Enter In,* you will realize that God is molding and developing a mighty woman of God in Deborah Stricklin. As Deborah has yielded to the purposes of God in her life, her ministry influence and open doors for preaching continue to increase exponentially. God is pouring fresh words through Deborah that will impart transformation into your life.

Get ready for God to speak to you through the spiritual principles you will glean from *Enter In.* The remainder of this foreword contains truths that Deborah will present in ten easy-to-read chapters. The most important truth is that friendship with God is the key for your transformation. Deborah skillfully writes about two Biblical figures who walked in friendship with the Lord and led two different generations of Israelites. The first, Moses, led the Israelites out of Egyptian bondage and through the wilderness, and his successor, Joshua, led the next generation into the Promised Land. If God can use Moses and Joshua, He can use you, too.

Moses walked in obedience to God despite doubts, confusion, and overwhelming odds against him. The preparation process was not easy, but God chose Moses, and he responded from a posture of humility and total abandonment to God. By continuing to say "yes" to Him, Moses set in motion a beautiful legacy of friendship with God.

Joshua was a man of faithfulness behind the scenes, and he demonstrated a heart focused on upholding another's vision. Perhaps the truest test of a leader is how they carry out the vision of another. Joshua never attempted to take his position as Israel's leader; he allowed God to determine when the time of transition had come. Like Moses, humility was a key factor to Joshua ultimately being transitioned into leadership as Moses' replacement. While patiently waiting, God is actively preparing your heart and positioning everything in place for what is to come. Transition can be difficult because it is a balancing act of what has been and what will be.

Whether walking through the battle of cancer with her mother or feeling confined as in a prison during a long season of waiting, Deborah will challenge you to walk with God through overwhelming circumstances and continue to trust Him when all seems lost. Regardless of the dream God has placed in your heart, you must understand that no God-dream is ever accomplished without battling giants and walking through dark valleys. Laying hold of God's promises never comes without a fight, and don't give up just because it's taking longer than you thought to see the fulfillment.

Deborah writes that our goal with our children is to mentor these selfish little rascals into adulthood with Christ-like character, Kingdom purpose, and dream-inspired vision. Likewise, that is exactly what God is doing in you. The question is will you be hesitant to obey, or will you walk forward with complete abandon and unquestioning trust? The goal is Christ-like character, Kingdom purpose, and dream-inspired vision. The reward is His friendship and His presence. You can grow through a lifestyle of faithfulness, commitment, obedience, and finishing well.

It's all about becoming a friend of God.

— Terry Bailey, Superintendent
Tennessee Assembly of God Ministry Network

Introduction

THE STORY OF MOSES and Joshua, as they led the people of Israel out of Egypt into the Promised Land, has always fascinated me. Why anyone would be so bought into the idea of taking charge of two million rebellious people is incredibly puzzling. Obviously, Moses was prepared by God, heard God's call, and walked in obedience toward God's plan of liberating His enslaved children. Moses' journey was characterized by many hardships and a lot of loneliness, but the weight of defending God's honor propelled him toward the goal of entering the Promised Land with all of those people in tow.

Although, along the way, Moses lost his privilege of crossing the threshold of that land, God raised up Joshua to finish what He had started. Joshua's journey was certainly one of obscurity until it was time to take possession of God's promise to His people. Yet, Joshua's faithfulness behind the scenes ushered him into the leadership role that established God's children in their land of blessing. Hard-fought battles characterized most of the rest of Joshua's life, but the people fought alongside their leader and remained faithful to God until Joshua's death.

When God offers *us* the opportunity to adventure with Him into the life of faith, hard-fought battles become common fare, and our faithfulness determines *how* we enter into His promised plan. This book, through recounting Moses' and Joshua's story, is a blueprint of sorts on the path toward God's purposed outcome in our lives. Opportunities, pitfalls, and victories lay ahead. And, at the center of it all, is the greatest victory—friendship with the God we grow to revere and honor through the process. No other outcome is sweeter or worth the price that is paid along the way.

CHAPTER ONE

Lofty Ambitions

MOSES' BIRTH CAME COMPLETE with God's miraculous stamp of approval. As the Israelites multiplied in Egypt, the new king of the land (who was generations removed from Joseph and his family) determined to reduce the Hebrew population by having all the newborn males killed. The Hebrew midwives, although ordered by Pharaoh to carry out the murders, feared God and refused to obey the king. With Pharaoh's plan thwarted, his anger grew to an unprecedented level. His new order was issued—throw all the newborn Israelite boys into the Nile River. Moses' parents chose to hide him, instead. He was born at the hands of uncompromising women and protected under the care of faithful parents. The liberation plan of God's people was now underway.

GOD'S ACTS OF LIBERATION ALWAYS BEGIN WITH THE CHOOSING OF A MAN OR A WOMAN THROUGH WHOM HE WILL CARRY OUT HIS PLAN.

God chose Moses. God's acts of liberation always begin with the choosing of a man or a woman through whom He will carry out His plan. Sometimes His Word indicates the reasoning behind His choice, but more often than not, we're left to wonder why He makes the choices He does. He's God, and we're not—pretty simple. God protected Moses through the first forty years of his life, allowing him to grow up under the leadership of the very regime that sought to end his infant life. Pharaoh's daughter plucked Moses' floating reed bed out of the Nile River and took him as her own. It's no insignificant detail that Moses' own mother was chosen to nurse Moses until he was old enough to live in the palace with Pharaoh's family. The Hebrew songs and prayers poured over him during his years of infancy planted seeds that yielded a necessary and unprecedented harvest in God's predetermined timing.

God also knew that Moses would need desert survival training before assuming the leadership role of parenting over two million people for forty long years in the wilderness. So, after a needless murder, Moses fled Pharaoh's vindictive pursuit, and the wilderness became Moses' home for the second forty-year phase of his life. The number forty characterizes each phase of Moses' life, and interestingly, the number forty means "testing upon the earth." Whether it was the testing of Moses' fortitude, the building of character, or the carrying out of punishment on God's children, forty year phases often marked the people and leadership of Israel. So, with Moses' desert training complete, he was ready to receive God's call.

The preparation process in *our* lives can be brutal. Just when we think life is looking pretty good, what has seemed secure comes unglued. And... not unglued in just one area, but in almost every area of our lives. God's leadership institute has one goal in mind—complete surrender and submission to His Lordship. He's not punishing us during this process; He's preparing us. It can be incredibly challenging to maintain the focus of preparation when it feels as if the onslaught will surely drown us. What's immensely comforting to me is that He doesn't require us to *enjoy* the painful parts of the process; He just asks us to allow the process to shape us. And, it is the decision of our will to lean into His beckoning. Accepting the position of humility and abandonment is our task, and that's no easy accomplishment. Daily, we fall to our knees and ask for help to position our hearts before Him. Years of faithful submission yield hearts that are fully prepared. God's season of preparation in our lives can span decades, as in King David's twenty-year journey to the throne or Joshua's forty-year sentence of wilderness wandering. Jesus' thirty years of preparation preceded His three years of ministry. And, Moses was no exception. The magnitude of his assignment required much preparation.

> GOD'S LEADERSHIP INSTITUTE HAS ONE GOAL IN MIND - COMPLETE SURRENDER AND SUBMISSION TO HIS LORDSHIP.

The day finally came when God decided Moses was ready to receive the instructions that would consume the rest of his life. The burning bush became the dividing line between preparation and execution. It was time.

One day Moses was tending the flock of his father-in-law, Jethro, the priest of Midian, and he went deep

> *into the wilderness near Sinai, the mountain of God. Suddenly, the angel of the LORD appeared to him as a blazing fire in a bush. Moses was amazed because the bush was engulfed in flames, but it didn't burn up. "Amazing!" Moses said to himself. "Why isn't that bush burning up? I must go over to see this." When the LORD saw that he had caught Moses' attention, God called to him from the bush, "Moses! Moses!" (Exodus 3:1-4, NLT)*

That phrase, *"When the LORD saw that he had caught Moses' attention,"* is incredibly significant. I sometimes wonder how long the Lord has to work at getting *our* attention. His quiet whispers go unnoticed, and His gentle nudges are dismissed. His beckoning through uncomfortable circumstances is interpreted as punishment rather than as a loving reminder. All the while, He is calling to us. But, are we listening? Notice that Moses was alone in the wilderness when God took advantage of this opportune moment. How often do we purposefully position ourselves in quiet solitude before our Father? Humanly speaking, if it took a walk through the wilderness and a flaming bush to arrest Moses' attention, we would do well to assume we're not just going to catch God's intentions toward us on the fly. We must be deliberate.

I SOMETIMES WONDER HOW LONG THE LORD HAS TO WORK AT GETTING OUR ATTENTION. HIS QUIET WHISPERS GO UNNOTICED, AND HIS GENTLE NUDGES ARE DISMISSED.

When my children were growing up, I instituted "quiet time." That term often connotes punishment or negative emotions. We're set apart from being with others because we somehow deserve separation. Unless someone interrupts this cycle of negativity toward separation, we grow up avoiding being alone. And, if we do find ourselves alone, we tend to fill our ears with everything except silence.

But, "quiet time" is actually a very positive and necessary discipline that we, as adults, would do well to implement in our lives. In my parenting, I was intentional about teaching my children the value of a quiet heart and mind. On the surface, it might appear that I assigned them to their rooms for my own sanity's sake (having three babies in a four year span gives some credence to preserving my sanity), but my main goal was to instill in them a longing for stillness and silence. As they grew, their appointed "quiet time" was age-appropriate. I only had two rules—They couldn't talk to one another, and they could only read, nap, write, or draw. I saw an incredible outcome begin to emerge as the years went by; they sought quiet time for themselves. It was as if moments of down-time became necessary to maintain a healthy spirit. And, as adults, they still seek those quiet moments of retreat. We will live better if we'll train ourselves to have a quiet heart. Perhaps we'll hear what we've been missing from the Spirit of God. He desires to adventure with us, and He waits for us to respond.

WE WILL LIVE BETTER IF WE'LL TRAIN OURSELVES TO HAVE A QUIET HEART.

Moses saw it, God's attention-grabbing mini inferno. His reply was simple and profound, *"Here I am!"* (Exodus 3:4, NLT). Moses didn't run from God; he waited to hear what God had to say. After identifying Himself and conveying the heart cry of His children, God gave Moses a directive, *"Now go, for I am sending you to Pharaoh. You will lead my people, the Israelites, out of Egypt"* (Exodus 3:10, NLT). That's an incredibly intimidating statement! Moses' reply was appropriate; *"But who am I to appear before Pharaoh?"* (Exodus 3:11, NLT). Sometimes we wonder if God has forgotten who He's talking to. I titled this chapter Lofty Ambitions, not regarding Moses' thoughts of himself, but of God's thoughts toward Moses. It seems rather audacious that God would ambitiously send a man from the wilderness to retrieve over two million people from the dictatorial hands of the world's most powerful leader. And, yet, God is completely confident about the idea.

OUR FRAGILITY NO LONGER MATTERS WHEN GOD IS ADDED TO THE EQUATION.

He often asks us to walk with Him into overwhelming circumstances and continue to trust Him when all looks lost. At those moments, we intimately feel our humanity and question if He has mistakenly assigned the task. But God's next statement to Moses dispels all misunderstanding. *"Then God told him, 'I will be with you'"* (Exodus 3:12, NLT). Our fragility no longer matters when God is added to the equation. What seemed impossibly overwhelming becomes plausible knowing that the King of Kings goes before us. He, who turns situations around, directs the hearts of kings, and causes nature to align with His purposes, is in charge; we're just a cooperating part of *His* plan.

There is such comfort in those words, *"I will be with you."* We are truly safe in the hands of the Father.

And, so begins Moses' incredible adventure with the God of the Universe. The Lord proceeds to give Moses specific instructions on approaching Pharaoh, words to speak and demands to make. God assigns Aaron as Moses' prophet, carrying out all that Moses hears from God. Pharaoh mocks them at first, dismissing their demands as a parent dismisses a child's unreasonable tirade. But, as God ups the ante, Pharaoh begins to wonder if this God Moses is representing *really can* carry out all these threats. God wasn't interested in just rescuing His people; He wanted the entire known world to know His power. And, He made sure Pharaoh's heart stayed hardened just long enough to display His indisputable might.

As we read through the book of Exodus, we learn to appreciate the yielded vessel Moses had become during the weeks God displayed His mighty power throughout Egypt. This was no easy task—confronting a world power, withstanding the mocking rebelliousness of Pharaoh, being derided by the people you were sent to rescue, and defending the name of an invisible God. And, yet, this is what God asks of us as well. In the hands of the Almighty, we become His incredibly powerful tool. But, our willingness to yield ourselves completely to the process is crucial for the exaltation of His name. Until the odds are against us while we are campaigning for Him, we're still working our *own* agenda. In that moment, when it's just God and us (with an impossible plan), our resolve is tested. Our trust in Him becomes the all-important factor in continuing on.

It seems to me that God has incredibly lofty ambitions for us; and I'm amazed that He would trust *us* to walk with Him into unimaginably great adventures. As I think about other adventurers such as Noah, Abraham, Joseph, Joshua, and David, my faith rises that God could use me, too, to leave an indelible mark on *my* generation and those yet to come. With each one of these heroes of Biblical proportion, they have something in common—they became friends of God. When you're willing to risk everything to take on giants with your invisible Force Field going before you, you become friends.

I'M AMAZED THAT HE WOULD TRUST US TO WALK WITH HIM INTO UNIMAGINABLY GREAT ADVENTURES.

God is so incredibly patient with us. He knows that to become His friend, we have to go through a transformational process. Our nature is so selfish, and we live badly until we've completely yielded to Him. At the moment we accept Jesus Christ as the Savior of our souls, we have made Him our God. Then, over time, and with the reading of His Word, we learn to make Him Lord. The yielding of our will to His is usually a lengthy and painstaking process, but once we've experienced the freedom in Him that comes with proper Lordship, we see the value of daily crucifixion. There is joy in obedience and a deep sense of satisfaction in willingly following Him. However, to stop at Lordship is to stop short of His ultimate goal. His desire is to walk and dream with His creation as friends.

There is no way to dwell in that friendship without going through the process of Lordship because a friend of God is a heart that wants His purposes accomplished and His majesty displayed. As His friend, we simply become His conduit to the dying humanity around us. His heart is never about exalting us; He wants our partnership in rescuing humanity and exalting His name, just like with Moses. This requires that we relinquish *our* desires to take on *His* desires, which is a daily exercise in humility!

The trust that is forged during this process of Lordship and friendship sustains us through the challenges that lay ahead. No God-dream is ever accomplished without battling giants and walking through dark valleys. But, with His presence, we prevail. With His companionship, we emerge stronger *because* of the battles. We often don't realize how strong we've grown through the sparring process. Our focus has been laser-like, warring our way through the long nights and hard-fought days. Long before we've won the war, others have begun to take notice that we're different, more confident somehow. And, then, once we've slain a giant or two, we begin to see our matured reflection. God has grown us. We've learned to walk with Him, and it's beautiful.

NO GOD-DREAM IS EVER ACCOMPLISHED WITHOUT BATTLING GIANTS AND WALKING THROUGH DARK VALLEYS.

CHAPTER TWO

Overwhelming Odds

When God speaks His purposes to us, we unreasonably expect Him to miraculously impose His will, carrying out His full directive. But, rarely does this happen in such a clean, linear fashion. Before Moses and Aaron approached Pharaoh, God gave Moses instructions about the miracles he was to perform in Pharaoh's presence. I imagine Moses was a little surprised when Pharaoh's wise men and magicians could mimic God's miracles. It would be easy to adopt a sense of inferiority as Pharaoh's magicians performed their similar tricks. But, Moses seemed to sense that God was building His case. In the end, there would be no contest; God would emerge the unquestionable champion.

When we launch in adventure with God, our sense of conquering against all odds is often premature. God is incredibly patient. All *we* want to do is hurry up and win because being on the winning team makes *us* look good! But, God has a much greater purpose in mind. Not only is He considering all who are watching, He is also stacking the odds against Himself to create a weightier impact at the moment of victory. Although God comes out looking like the God He is in the end, *we* tend to deal with feelings of insecurity, inferiority, and injustice before it's all said and done. The main reason—limited vision. God sees all the way to the end of the situation, positions each player for maximum impact, and creates scenarios along the way for His name to be exalted. God told Moses,

> *I will cause Pharaoh to be stubborn so I can multiply my miraculous signs and wonders in the land of Egypt. Even then Pharaoh will refuse to listen to you. So I will crush Egypt with a series of disasters, after which I will lead the forces of Israel out with great acts of judgment. When I show the Egyptians my power and force them to let the Israelites go, they will realize that I am the LORD. (Exodus 3-5, NLT)*

GOD SEES ALL THE WAY TO THE END OF THE SITUATION.

One by one, the ten plagues heralded God's presence and power. And, just before the plague of hail, God sent this message to Pharaoh through Moses,

> *I will prove to you that there is no other God like me in all the earth. I could have killed you by now. I could have attacked you with a plague that would have wiped you from the face of the earth. But I have let you live for this reason—that you might see my power and that my fame might spread throughout the earth. (Exodus 9:14-16, NLT)*

I always wondered, as a child, why the Bible kept saying that God hardened Pharaoh's heart throughout the exodus story. It just didn't seem right that God set up Pharaoh to fail. Eventually, I saw it—that God knew Pharaoh's heart from the beginning and used the situation to exalt His own name and free His people with quite a bang. The surrounding people groups would fear Him and His children, and Israel would pass down the incredible stories for all generations yet to be born.

The part of this story we don't highlight enough is Moses' willingness to walk with God through the doubt, confusion, and overwhelming odds. The fact that Moses responded to God, traveled back to Egypt (knowing he would have to face his past), stand before Pharaoh, be ridiculed by both the Egyptians and the Hebrews, and look foolish until the last scene deserves just a little bit of credit. As I said earlier, when God chooses to carry out an act of liberation, He always prepares a man or woman to work through. The beauty (and challenge) of God partnering with us is the human will. We have the choice to let God have His way in us or choose to ignore His directives. The latter certainly has its consequences (dying short of walking in our designed purpose is best case scenario), but I want to focus on celebrating the choice to let God have His way in us.

MOSES SET IN MOTION A BEAUTIFUL LEGACY OF FRIENDSHIP WITH GOD BY CONTINUALLY SAYING YES.

Moses made the hard choices to keep letting God lead him. The idea of legacy is little more than passing on something significant or valuable. It could be a talent or gift. It could be the gift of handling large sums of money. Or, it could be the choices of obedience toward God. We'll delve into the focus of legacy more in the last chapter of this book, but we'll say, for now, Moses set in motion a beautiful legacy of friendship with God by continually saying yes. Moses chose to trust God even when nothing seemed to be going God's way. Each plague was imposed; Pharaoh looked like he would cave in to Moses' demands, and then this stubborn king exerted his refusal. God may have appeared to be losing the battle, but with the last plague (the death of Egypt's firstborn) the tables were turned. God gave Moses these instructions,

> *"I will send just one more disaster on Pharaoh and the land of Egypt. After that, Pharaoh will let you go. In fact, he will be so anxious to get rid of you that he will practically force you to leave the country. Tell all the Israelite men and women to ask their Egyptian neighbors for articles of silver and gold." (Now the LORD had caused the Egyptians to look favorably on the people of Israel, and Moses was considered a very great man in the land of Egypt. He was respected by Pharaoh's officials and the Egyptian people alike.) (Exodus 11:1-3, NLT)*

WHEN GOD PLACES A DREAM OR CALLING IN OUR HEARTS, THE DECIDING FACTOR IS WHETHER WE'LL BELIEVE HIM.

And God further instructed, *"Pharaoh will not listen to you. But this will give me the opportunity to do even more mighty miracles in the land of Egypt"* (Exodus 12:9, NLT). Moses believed God. It's that simple. Through all of the events from the burning bush to the parting of the Red Sea, Moses believed God. No matter the odds, Moses had his eyes on his Lord. When God places a dream or calling in our hearts, the deciding factor is whether we'll believe Him. If we do, we find strength and courage in keeping our eyes glued to Him during the ensuing roller coaster ride as He creates situations for His name to be lifted up. We may look foolish along the way for believing what He has told us, but in the end, those who chided us will wish they hadn't.

As the death angel passed over Egypt, Pharaoh's eldest son died. In his grief, Pharaoh told the Israelites to get out of his presence, and the children of God left Egypt weighed down with gifts from the Egyptians who were hoping to pacify this all-powerful God. Although Pharaoh exerted one last effort to subdue the people by chasing them into the Red Sea, he was humbled into submission by the drowning of his army. God won, hands down. Moses emerged as God's great liberating tool, all because Moses believed and obeyed Him. Although Moses didn't *earn* God's approval, his decisions positioned him to be used by God.

This is such a critical point... We are the decision makers. We have a will, and our choices before the Lord either give us the opportunity to be used by Him or, like Pharaoh, to be left behind and unusable in His Kingdom. Somehow, we've adopted the idea that both decisions have equal weight—choosing to yield to Him or choosing to continue our current lifestyle. The *fear of the Lord* ought to curb our self-fulfilling lives, but in many ways, we've lost that, too. I don't know how else to seize the attention of sleeping Christians other than to live full-out for the God who deserves my highest praise and every moment of my life.

I have nothing of more worth to offer Him than my life, so that's what I will give. My decisions toward Him are, "Yes." They will keep being, "Yes." Through moments of victory, through moments of seeming defeat, through moments of humility, and through moments of overwhelming odds, my answer to Him is, "Yes."

It's a question of value. What do you value more—your own desires or your soul? Jesus made the choice clear in Mark 8:34-37,

> *Then he called his disciples and the crowds to come over and listen, "If any of you wants to be my follower," he told them, "you must put aside your selfish ambition, shoulder your cross, and follow me. If you try to keep your life for yourself, you will lose it. But if you give up your life for my sake and for the sake of the Good News, you will find true life. And how do you benefit if you gain the whole world but lose your own soul in the process? Is anything worth more than your soul?" (NLT)*

GIVE UP THE RIGHTS TO YOUR OWN LIFE.

So, why do we have a tendency to choose badly? Fear, pride, and unbelief probably top the list. The solution is simple—give up. Give up the rights to your own life. Turn them over to God. We're investing in eternity. This life is so short compared to our eternity with Him.

Where our focus is determines our choices. If we're focused on the here and now, we'll make self-fulfilling decisions. If we're focused on eternity, we'll make self-denying decisions. I'm looking toward the reward, knowing that my life here is my investment opportunity. Choose to trust Him. Choose to believe Him. Choose to dream with Him. Nothing this world has to offer even comes close to the beauty of partnering with the God who designed us to adventure with Him.

One of the most detrimental hindrances to abandoning ourselves before the Lord is *earthly position.* Our flesh enjoys position, and pride can easily rise because of it. In the church, holding positions of leadership can sometimes blind people to remaining completely open and vulnerable before the Lord. It's challenging to maintain an attitude of service and humility before the Father while standing in a position that is held in high esteem before people. It is wise that our conduct be filtered through the grid of how we will be seen by those we lead, but we must be cautious that our highest goal is a rightly positioned heart before the Father, not before men. Perhaps the truest test is when God asks us to step away from a position for a time. Will we obey? We often equate position with influence. But, the beauty of influence is that it isn't limited by or to position. We could be title-less and be incredibly influential. Our humility before God brings *His* favor, which creates influence. Don't worry about whether you have a position or not; actually, there's a lot of freedom in influence without position. Seek His heart, and follow Him wholeheartedly; influence will come as a (super) natural by-product.

OUR HUMILITY BEFORE GOD BRINGS HIS FAVOR, WHICH CREATES INFLUENCE.

Although Moses faced overwhelming odds against Pharaoh actually releasing his two-million-strong labor force, Moses kept His eyes and ears focused on God. He was able to be led by God through the maze of false appearances. *Our* challenge is keep our eyes on Jesus and remain focused on His instructions to us even in the face of overwhelming odds.

My family has been walking through the battle of cancer with my mom for about a year now. Her first round with the diagnosis seemed to be resolved through surgery, however, its angry vengeance resurfaced recently leaving her body riddled with the disease. The toughest part of the battle hasn't been physical; it's been mentally obtaining a focused will to live. I love my mom's desire to be with Jesus. All my life, it seems she has barely lived in this world. Her eyes have always been focused on Jesus and eternity with Him. So, this bout with cancer seemingly presented her with her ticket home. The "problem" has been that God is not finished with her here yet. That means, despite the overwhelming odds in front of her, she must choose to remain engaged here until the day the Father decides it's time for her to come home. She has chosen to focus on her intended purpose rather than the disease.

THERE IS SOMETHING ABOUT THE ACT OF CROSSING THE THRESHOLD THAT IS SACRED TO US.

Every day is another opportunity to bring glory to the One who stood in the gap for us and is providing an eternal home prepared for those who choose Him. One day, we will each cross the threshold of Heaven! That is certainly a day to look forward to with great joy. There is something about the act of crossing the threshold that is sacred to us—bringing our newborn baby home for the first time, entering our own home as newlyweds, coming home from a long trip, or returning home alone for the first time after the death of a loved one. Home provides a place of refuge from our storms, and the joy of returning there comforts our weary hearts. Heaven will one day soon be our forever-home. Until then, we must face the overwhelming odds of this life with an attitude of praise for the One who turns the odds in His favor every time! You're on the winning side; don't let any of life's circumstances tell you otherwise.

CHAPTER THREE

Courageous Loneliness

ONE OF THE MOST common aspects of leadership can be loneliness. Decisions are often made at the expense of popularity, and a leader's personal sacrifice is easily overlooked by those they lead. Courage, then, is required to step into a leadership role when summoned—courage to stand alone when necessary and courage to absorb the blows of criticism and the adulation of conditional praise. Perhaps it is beneficial to be blissfully unaware of some of the inevitable conflicts that lay ahead for most leaders. I am very sure Moses had no idea what he was getting into when God told him to serve as the intermediary between Pharaoh and Himself.

A LEADER'S PERSONAL SACRIFICE IS EASILY OVERLOOKED BY THOSE THEY LEAD.

The people wasted no time initiating complaints against Moses. When Moses the liberator first arrived on the scene, Pharaoh responded to Moses' demands by making the people work harder. Their response? *"May the LORD judge you for getting us into this terrible situation with Pharaoh and his officials"* (Exodus 5:21, NLT). There isn't a lot of gratitude for Moses' leadership in those words. Even after Moses led them out of Pharaoh's presence, the people easily abandoned any trust they may have developed in him. *"Our Egyptian slavery was far better than dying out here in the wilderness!"* (Exodus 14:12, NLT). This chant became the people's mantra any time they experienced threat or discomfort. They were incredibly forgetful of their misery in slavery and God's constant intervention. Moses often had to deal with this unyielding, complaining spirit among two million people over the next forty years.

LEADERSHIP, WHEN TAKEN SERIOUSLY, IS LESS ABOUT BEING IN CHARGE AND MORE ABOUT ALLOWING GOD TO MOLD US TO FIT HIS PURPOSES IN SERVING OTHERS.

Leadership, when taken seriously, is less about being in charge and more about allowing God to mold us to fit His purposes in serving others. God's ultimate purpose in Moses' leadership was to prepare these complaining children to be His beacon of light to the world. God was calling them to a higher purpose, and Moses was appointed to show them the way. What an awesome responsibility leaders have to serve as a launching pad for others' success!

It's the responsibility of leaders to equip those surrounding them to walk in God's purpose for their lives. Although there are many philosophies about leadership styles, there is only one style we need to emulate. Christ's leadership style was demonstrated by humbling Himself in order to provide those He led the opportunity to have life in all of its fullness. Many leaders, even in our churches, see their roles as positions of power rather than people development opportunities. But, in Mark 10:43-45, Jesus made it clear that being a leader equals the greatest act of servanthood,

> *Whoever wants to be a leader among you must be your servant, and whoever wants to be first must be the slave of all. For even I, the Son of Man, came here not to be served but to serve others, and to give my life as a ransom for many (NLT).*

Jesus never held a position of power during His three years of ministry; He did, however, create the greatest impact this world has ever known. George O. Wood, in His devotional *Fearless*, said, "Greatness is how you care for the people who don't have position, wealth, title, or office." So, leadership becomes a platform by which we support others and lift them higher, not a throne by which we command authority.

JESUS MADE IT CLEAR THAT BEING A LEADER EQUALS THE GREATEST ACT OF SERVANTHOOD.

Probably one of the most difficult exercises for leaders is keeping *people* prioritized above *task*. Many leaders are naturally a type-A temperament, which means they're goal-oriented go-getters. In going after a goal, no matter how noble it might be, these world-changers sometimes lose sight of people along the way.

It's easy to be so focused on the goal that you don't see the people around you. Many times, if a person isn't directly beneficial to the goal, they get overlooked. Not that they're intentionally ignored, they just aren't seen as pertinent at the moment. But, people are always supposed to be the main goal. And, a perspective shift is definitely in order! My mom has always said, "The problem with your perspective is that it's the only one you've got." Our need, then, to see situations from God's perspective becomes paramount. And, from *His* perspective, people always take priority over task.

How we view people determines how we proceed. If we can begin to see the people around us as potential difference-makers, we start recognizing their value. We become their cheerleaders and facilitators. Their success becomes our joy. And, when other people's hopes and dreams become more important to us than our own, we're finally seeing from God's perspective.

> LEADERSHIP BECOMES A PLATFORM BY WHICH WE SUPPORT OTHERS AND LIFT THEM HIGHER, NOT A THRONE BY WHICH WE COMMAND AUTHORITY.

Many people will respond to this kind of positive input and succeed in pursuing their purpose. However, not everyone will. No matter how much encouragement is provided, some folks are bent on seeing the negative side of things. I'm amazed at the number of times Moses had to step between the people and God's wrath. The people were obstinate and complaining. I think I would have stepped aside and let the lightning bolts fly! But, not Moses; he even reminded God that His own reputation was at stake if He annihilated the very people He just delivered. Great perspective! Leaders often have to travel the road of long-term commitment with difficult followers. It's simply part of the job. But, over the long haul, if leaders are paying attention, they'll discover the hidden gems God has entrusted them to lead. There will be a few followers who will emerge as future leaders with great energy to learn and grow. Some people are (super) naturally hungry for the things of the Lord. Joshua was one of these hidden gems that Moses led to greatness. Before all was said and done, Joshua would be the one chosen to lead God's children into the Promised Land.

Who among us is God's next chosen vessel? If we'll see ourselves as gem-finders, our eyes will be off ourselves and onto others. Somehow, as we're helping others succeed, God brings us the success in His Kingdom we've been longing for. Our success is always tied up in the promotion of others.

WE HOARD RESPONSIBILITY, AS IF OUR WORTH IS DETERMINED BY HOW MUCH WE MUST DO.

Sometimes we hoard responsibility, as if our worth is determined by how much we must do. It seems that, over time, accumulation just happens, and we end up with the lion's share of tasks. There's an answer for this situation—Delegate! (Not just for the purpose of making less work for ourselves, but for the purpose of empowering others to participate in the work and discover their own latent abilities.) Moses' father-in-law, Jethro, gave him advice that is helpful to us as well.

The next day, Moses sat as usual to hear the people's complaints against each other. They were lined up in front of him from morning till evening. When Moses' father-in-law saw all that Moses was doing for the people, he said, "Why are you trying to do all this alone? The people have been standing here all day to get your help." Moses replied, "Well, the people come to me to seek God's guidance. When an argument arises, I am the one who settles the case. I inform the people of God's decisions and teach them his laws and instructions." "This is not good!" his father-in-law exclaimed. "You're going to wear yourself out—and the people, too. This job is too heavy a burden for you to handle all by yourself. Now let me give you a word of advice, and may God be with you. You should continue to be the people's representative before God, bringing him their questions to be decided. You should tell them God's decisions, teach them God's laws and instructions, and show them how to conduct their lives. But find some capable, honest men who fear God and hate bribes. Appoint them as judges over groups of one thousand, one hundred, fifty, and ten. These men can serve the people, resolving all the ordinary cases. Anything that is too important or too complicated can be brought to you. But they can take care of the smaller matters themselves. They will help you carry the load, making the task easier for you. If you follow this advice, and if God directs you to do so, then you will be able to endure the pressures, and all these people will go home in peace." Moses listened to his father-in-law's advice and followed his suggestions. (Exodus 18:13-24, NLT)

How many times have we found ourselves lamenting over being burdened with the day-to-day tasks that *could* be done by others? The perfectionist in us wants each task done a certain way, to the point that we can't bring ourselves to hand it off to a capable person. So, we hoard.

We keep what doesn't belong to us and become dysfunctional because we couldn't bring ourselves to delegate. Let's be honest—we're being selfish and prideful when we don't delegate. We don't think others can do a good job with *our* task, and we like feeling indispensable. We are self-focused and isolative when we hoard. Our job as leaders is to train and empower others. Yes, training and empowering others takes time and can be a little messy. We must be prepared for their mistakes and failures, but these are part of the learning process and part of our training responsibility. Remember the focus is on people, not tasks. So, we concern ourselves less with the perfection of the task than the development of the person. This is a mindset shift—a perspective change. But, until we, as leaders, make the shift, we limit ourselves and the capacity of our leadership. We can only handle so many tasks, but as we empower others to work alongside us, the load becomes light, and people begin to step into the participation of teamwork.

LET'S BE HONEST – WE'RE BEING SELFISH AND PRIDEFUL WHEN WE DON'T DELEGATE.

Pastors tend to struggle greatly with this concept because the seriousness of the work seems too fragile to hand off to others. The beauty of delegation is the growth we see in those who assume new roles of authority. This transfer of authority involves trust that God is helping us oversee the work of His Kingdom within our sphere. God wants His children to link arms, see each other's value, and serve His Kingdom as a team. We have no other reasonable choice than to empower fellow believers. We should see our leadership role as a privileged opportunity to develop the gifts and talents of our brothers and sisters in Christ. As we view others as valuable assets to the Kingdom of God, we begin a fulfilling journey of legacy in our own lives. (We'll dive into legacy in more depth in the last chapter of this book.)

For decades, the identity of the church has been centralized in our church buildings. People who found themselves in despair or stuck in difficult situations in life would seek answers by walking into a local church building. We, as believers, would then minister to the person and welcome them into our church family. This dynamic of church identity is changing in our current generation. The church is being somewhat decentralized. Instead of people coming to our church buildings, we are being commissioned to go to them. Because there is a growing lack of natural gravitation toward the church buildings, we must individually internalize the message of Jesus Christ and take it into our spheres of influence. We must become a walking version of the Word. This requires that we own the truth of the Bible—all of it! We no longer rely on the Sunday message to be our main meal; we must feed ourselves on God's Word. We witness. We testify. We pray for others. And, we invite them to join us as we gather for corporate fellowship, worship, and equipping. Then, we go out again.

AS WE VIEW OTHERS AS VALUABLE ASSETS TO THE KINGDOM OF GOD, WE BEGIN A FULFILLING JOURNEY OF LEGACY IN OUR OWN LIVES.

We've gotten lazy, letting our pastors do all the work. We go about our week, come to church for a good sermon and some inspiring songs, and go back to our daily routines. This has become detrimental to us as the Body of Christ and ineffective to the world around us. Digging into the Word, owning the Truth, and walking in the power of Holy Spirit is the only way to effectively bring the Gospel message to a world who no longer has an accurate compass for truth. Breaking up the holy huddle takes courage, but being the Light of the Gospel in the places of the broken and the unlovely is incredibly fulfilling.

God doesn't call
the qualified....
3/28/18 He qualifies the Called!!

CHAPTER FOUR

The Long Road of Obscurity

I ADMIRE JOSHUA. We see his true colors as he returns with the eleven scouts from spying out the Promised Land. Joshua and his fellow traveler, Caleb, are full of faith to possess the land, but the other ten scouts withdraw in fear. Not only are the ten fearful, they incite others to doubt God's promise and turn against Joshua, Caleb, and Moses. The Israelites' ensuing unbelief then catapults them into forty years of wandering while those who spoke against the promise died in the wilderness. Joshua and Caleb would, at the end of forty years, be the only ones from that generation to enter the land that God had promised to give His children.

Joshua's faith is nothing short of beautiful. It's admirable enough that he believed when others didn't, but during those forty years of waiting to enter the land, he continued to grow into the leader God would use to replace His servant, Moses. The humility and consistency required to maintain a leader's focus during so many years of obscurity is worthy of our attention.

Our first glimpse of Joshua came prior to scouting out the land. While the Israelites were trekking between the exodus from Egypt and their arrival at Mount Sinai, they camped at a place called Rephidim. There, they were attacked.

> *While the people of Israel were still at Rephidim, the warriors of Amalek came to fight against them. Moses commanded Joshua, "Call the Israelites to arms, and fight the army of Amalek. Tomorrow, I will stand at the top of the hill with the staff of God in my hand." So Joshua did what Moses had commanded. He led his men out to fight the army of Amalek. Meanwhile Moses, Aaron, and Hur went to the top of a nearby hill. As long as Moses held up the staff with his hands, the Israelites had the advantage. But, whenever he lowered his hands, the Amalekites gained the upper hand. Moses' arms finally became too tired to hold up the staff any longer. So Aaron and Hur found a stone for him to sit on. Then they stood on each side, holding up his hands until sunset. As a result, Joshua and his troops were able to crush the army of Amalek. Then the LORD instructed Moses, "Write this down as a permanent record, and announce it to Joshua: I will blot out every trace of Amalek from under heaven." Moses built an altar there and called it "The LORD is My Banner." He said, "They have dared to raise their fist against the LORD's throne, so now the LORD will be at war with Amalek generation after generation." (Exodus 17:8-16, NLT)*

These audacious warriors of Amalek didn't have a clue what they were getting into when they decided to attack the children of God. Known for their hostility, the Amalekites would attack weaker tribes for both pleasure and profit. I can imagine that the Israelites (ex-slaves) seemed like easy sport. But, God protects those He calls His own! Moses assigned his go-to leader, Joshua, to rally the troops and fight. During the battle, Joshua's victory was dependent upon Moses keeping his staff raised above his head. There, on the hill, Moses remained all day with his arms stretched toward heaven holding the staff representing God's presence and power.

As leaders, we are truly dependent on one another. We tend to believe that we are more independent than we *ought* to think. But, our strength is in knowing that we work better together as a team. As servants of the Master, we function under one Headship, with one primary objective—to advance *His* Kingdom. Whether we are leaders within the ranks of the marketplace or leaders within the Church, we, as His Body, move in the same direction with one common goal. As we try to distinguish *ourselves,* we pull away from the established ranks, causing division rather than unity. Any breach in the ranks weakens the overall campaign. Joshua's job was to carry out the orders given him by Moses, although the battle was not won or lost at Joshua's hand. Moses' obedience to keep his hands upraised toward his Master was the solidification of God's intervention. So, Moses kept the staff raised, Aaron and Hur uplifted Moses' arms, Joshua motivated the troops to keep fighting, and *God* caused Amalek's defeat. God could

GOD PROTECTS THOSE HE CALLS HIS OWN!

have fought the battle all by Himself, but He desired the cooperation of His children one with another.

It's hard for us to depend on each other. We, as leaders, think we can accomplish tasks better ourselves than involving the people around us. Perhaps we can, but that's not the point. To be Kingdom minded is to be interdependent. Unfortunately, many of our churches have adopted a territorial mindset, especially in the Western world. We want to be distinguished as bigger, more prosperous, better attended, and more influential than our competitors (I mean colleagues). But, our greatest strength lies in linking arms with one another. The atmospheres, strongholds, and cultures of cities and regions could be completely transformed by the combined forces of God's kids, and yet, we act like selfish children trying to defend our self-declared kingdoms. It's time we stop declaring the boundaries of our turf and ride the brand of the larger Kingdom of God.

TO BE KINGDOM MINDED IS TO BE INTERDEPENDENT.

The generation that is now entering adulthood has been characterized as highly relational. They lean toward connecting emotionally and communicatively with each other. They aren't focused on who is out front or who gets the credit. Their main goal is rallying around a common interest, one that matters. Purpose, authenticity, and teamwork are all high priority. Older folks may see their social interconnectedness as a drawback or a distraction, but I don't think so. Perhaps God is preparing them for the necessary teamwork that is on the horizon of His Kingdom. These young adults are poised for an attitude of cooperation and unity within His Body as we've not yet seen in our lifetime. It's time. It's needed. It's imperative we join in.

And, I love how God gave a nod toward Joshua's future at the conclusion of the battle with the Amalekites. "*Then the LORD instructed Moses, 'Write this down as a permanent record, and announce it to Joshua: I will blot out every trace of Amalek from under heaven.'*" The scouting trip had not yet happened, and none of the people knew they'd be desert wanderers for the next forty years. But, God knew Joshua would need these instructions for the days of battle yet ahead. In the future, Joshua would be the one who would spearhead the Promised Land battles, expelling the godless people groups, and God instructed him never to concede toward those who He had declared His enemy.

Those forty years of waiting for his generation to die before he and the others could enter the Promised Land had to be difficult for Joshua. I imagine feelings of futility and frustration characterized some of those four decades. After all, all this waiting wasn't his doing. I wonder, if the people had been repentant during their desert experience rather than complaining, whether God would have relented and allowed them to go in. But, that wasn't the case, and the full sentence was served.

During his long years of obscurity in the desert under Moses' leadership, Joshua practiced the art of serving. Until we learn to serve well, God knows we won't lead well. In serving Moses, Joshua gained a heart focused on upholding another's vision. It's good for us, too, to put our own opinions aside about how something could be done differently and simply do our leader's bidding.

When we aren't the one in charge, it's not our call. We simply ask how we may serve and do it well.

Perhaps the truest test of a leader is how they carry out the vision of another. Leaders are, by nature, decision makers, and it is quite tempting to take the assignment given and make "improvements" along the way. The problem is that the fulfilled assignment (with its "improvements") might not match the original vision. Now, instead of serving, we have usurped our leader by adjusting the vision. I realize this sounds a little dramatic, but there is an attitude behind the action that needs adjustment. Feeling the need to make an assignment fit *your* expectations is a subtle form of control. And, a leader who controls is not a leader who walks in love. Ultimately, this points back to how we carry out the will of our Heavenly Father—Do we act according to His Word, or do we choose to adapt His edicts to our opinions and desires?

PERHAPS THE TRUEST TEST OF A LEADER IS HOW THEY CARRY OUT THE VISION OF ANOTHER.

What about remaining in the shadow of another when we feel we're fully capable of standing in their place of authority? Again, an attitude of control will attempt to seize the position or draw attention away from it, but an attitude of love will allow God to position people when He sees fit. And, remaining as one who serves the leader is truly a place of honor. Joshua never attempted to take his position as Israel's leader; he allowed God to determine when the time of transition had come. The willingness to serve well and remain in obscurity until the time is right is a beautiful act of humility that God blesses. Joshua passed this test of humility with flying colors. I desperately want the same to be said of me.

Our revered Bible hero, David, had the situation of usurped authority occur within his kingdom—by his own son no less! David had many children by many wives, an act of disobedience that cost him and his kingdom greatly throughout the generations to come. Absalom was David's third-born son. Amnon, Absalom's half-brother, raped Tamar, Absalom's sister. David didn't punish Amnon, perhaps because David saw all of this family drama as the fulfilled prediction of suffering rooted in his adulterous affair with Bathsheba (see 2 Samuel 12:11-12). Whatever David's reason, Absalom made his own bad choices and allowed his anger over the situation to turn to bitterness. Absalom killed Amnon, fled Jerusalem for three years, and then was allowed to return only to find that his father refused to see him for another two years. The bitterness in his soul became a breeding ground for revenge. As we pick up the story in 2 Samuel 15:1-12, we see that Absalom spent the next four years connivingly winning the hearts of the people, drawing their attention away from David and toward himself.

> A LEADER WHO CONTROLS IS NOT A LEADER WHO WALKS IN LOVE.

After this, Absalom bought a chariot and horses, and he hired fifty footmen to run ahead of him. He got up early every morning and went out to the gate of the city. When people brought a case to the king for judgment,

> *Absalom would ask where they were from, and they would tell him their tribe. Then Absalom would say, "You've really got a case here! It's too bad the king doesn't have anyone to hear it. I wish I were the judge. Then people could bring their problems to me, and I would give them justice!" And when people tried to bow before him, Absalom wouldn't let them. Instead, he took them by the hand and embraced them. So in this way, Absalom stole the hearts of all the people of Israel. After four years, Absalom said to the king, "Let me go to Hebron to offer a sacrifice to the LORD in fulfillment of a vow I made to him. For while I was at Geshur, I promised to sacrifice to him in Hebron if he would bring me back to Jerusalem." "All right," the king told him. "Go and fulfill your vow." So Absalom went to Hebron. But while he was there, he sent secret messengers to every part of Israel to stir up a rebellion against the king. "As soon as you hear the trumpets," his message read, "you will know that Absalom has been crowned king in Hebron." He took two hundred men from Jerusalem with him as guests, but they knew nothing of his intentions. While he was offering the sacrifices, he sent for Ahithophel, one of David's counselors who lived in Giloh. Soon many others also joined Absalom, and the conspiracy gained momentum. (NLT)*

David and his household were forced to flee Jerusalem for a time as Absalom attempted to usurp the throne. Eventually, Absalom was killed, and David returned to Jerusalem. Absalom had access to all that David had as a son of the king, but his embittered rage over the injustice toward his sister and David's inaction caused him to vie for his father's power, positioning himself as David's enemy.

No one would argue that injustice was done or that David mishandled the situation, but Absalom's lack of integrity emerged after nine years of stewing over the problem. At initial glance, Absalom would have made a good king. His outward appearance and people skills gave the impression of a good leader, but he lacked inner character and self-control.

Watching how someone handles injustice and long periods of waiting in subordinate positions is a good indicator of what is inside them. Will they wait for God to elevate them at the proper time, or will their impatience cause them to grab for position that isn't theirs for the taking? Humility is the key. Humility cautions us to be still in the Lord's presence as He works out circumstances according to His purposes. Fear will cause us to grab at what seems to elude us. If we already hold position, fear will cause us to cling to that which God is ready to transition. We must trust His timing. As we continue to see ourselves as His servants, He is able to use us in whatever capacity we currently occupy. Whether we lead from an established position or simply from influence, humility and character should guide our words and actions.

WATCHING HOW SOMEONE HANDLES INJUSTICE AND LONG PERIODS OF WAITING IN SUBORDINATE POSITIONS IS A GOOD INDICATOR OF WHAT IS INSIDE THEM.

CHAPTER FIVE

Painful Transition

TRANSITIONS CAN BE DIFFICULT. Emotional attachment causes us to be slow in opening our hand to the next season God brings our direction. We grow comfortable where we're at and shy away from the new unknown. And, in Moses' case, God told him he had to die and allow Joshua to lead Israel into the land promised to His children. That's rough.

It had been forty years since Moses led the people out of Egypt. Their desert wanderings were almost complete, and yet, their complaining remained. With no water, the people blamed Moses for their plight and yearned to be back in their land of slavery. In response,

> *Moses and Aaron turned away from the people and went to the entrance of the tabernacle, where they fell face down on the ground. Then the glorious presence of the LORD appeared to them, and the LORD said to Moses, "You and Aaron must take the staff and assemble the entire community. As the people watch, command the rock over there to pour out its water.*

> *You will get enough water from the rock to satisfy all the people and their livestock." (Numbers 20:6-8, NLT)*

Moses and Aaron were to stand before the people as God's representatives and command the rock to provide for the people. In the Scriptures that follow, it appears that Moses and Aaron let anger get the best of them.

> *So Moses did as he was told. He took the staff from the place where it was kept before the LORD. Then he and Aaron summoned the people to come and gather at the rock. "Listen, you rebels!" he shouted. "Must we bring water from this rock?" Then Moses raised his hand and struck the rock twice with the staff, and water gushed out. So all the people and their livestock drank their fill. But the LORD said to Moses and Aaron, "Because you did not trust me enough to demonstrate my holiness to the people of Israel, you will not lead them into the land I am giving them!" This place was known as the waters of Meribah, because it was where the people of Israel argued with the LORD, and where he demonstrated his holiness among them. (Numbers 20:9-13, NLT)*

Instead of following God's directive fully, Moses, in his anger, criticized the people, *struck* the rock twice, and took credit for God's miracle (*"Must* we *bring you water from this rock?")*. Our honest question to God is, "Is this really deserving of death?" But, we don't get to make those judgments. Moses was God's representative to an entire nation, and God held him to a standard we don't necessarily understand.

God's statement to Moses and Aaron, *"Because you did not trust me enough to demonstrate my holiness to the people of Israel..."* is an attention-stopper. I went to *Matthew Henry's Concise Commentary of the Whole Bible* to get a clearer perspective on God's words. What does it mean to neglect to demonstrate His holiness to the people? Henry puts it this way, "...they did not sanctify God, that is, they did not give to him alone that glory of this miracle which was due unto his name. And being provoked by the people, Moses (spoke) unadvisedly with his lips. The same pride of man would still usurp the office of the Mediator; and become to ourselves wisdom, righteousness, and sanctification, and redemption. Such a state of sinful independence, such a rebellion of the soul against its Saviour, the voice of God condemns in every page of the gospel." Wow! Those words are powerful—"The same pride of man would still usurp the office of the Mediator." We talked in the last chapter about usurping authority through applying our own twist on our leader's directives. This is exactly what Moses did. He put God on his own level by taking credit for the miracle and changing the way he carried out God's orders. Even further, to "usurp the office of the Mediator" is, in effect, to remove the only connection Moses had between his sinful humanity and the Almighty, Holy, and Righteous God. This is the same rebellion of any of mankind who would refuse the offering of the salvation of our Savior. Now, we understand

THE DEPTH OF OUR HUMANITY EXPOSES NOTHING BUT REBELLIOUS INDEPENDENCE FROM OUR CREATOR.

why Moses had to die. Now, we are amazed at the incredible love and grace that was extended by God to Moses in remaining friends. The depth of our humanity exposes nothing but rebellious independence from our Creator. Moses, in a moment of human error, failed to demonstrate before the people the honor, indisputable power, and majesty of our only Living Hope. What we do and what we say matters.

As we lead people, from position and/or influence, we don't have the luxury of reacting according to our emotions. Our outbursts may not come with a death sentence, but they cost us. We lose leadership equity among the people we lead when we act badly. We mistreat God's children when we don't stop to think and humble our hearts. Words escape our mouths that self-control ought to have held in. Facial expressions reveal pent-up bitterness and anger. We don't realize that we have the ability to demean and criticize with a look (or do we?). If we deliberately withhold a smile from someone, we are expressing our disapproval of them. That's arrogant! There's a difference between having a serious conversation with one who is sinning to bring repentance versus expressing disapproval of the person through *our* behavior. There's a controlling spirit at work in that situation, and it needs to be addressed. Criticism and joy can't share the same heart. I would rather smile at everyone and let God work out the ills in others' lives than go around choosing who I believe deserves or doesn't deserve *my* approval. Kindness is to rule our interactions as Christians.

WE LOSE LEADERSHIP EQUITY AMONG THE PEOPLE WE LEAD WHEN WE ACT BADLY.

We also don't realize what opportunities we may have lost due to mishandling our leadership roles. God may let an opportunity pass by us if we didn't handle the last one well. But, remember that God's love for us isn't fickle; He regards our humanity but never allows it to affect His love. Although Moses had to relinquish *his* privilege of entering the Promised Land, God still called him His friend. This is so beautiful! God never stopped loving Moses and didn't negate the friendship because of Moses' sinful act. Moses simply couldn't experience the fulfillment of the promise. It was God's justice for this situation.

CRITICISM AND JOY CAN'T SHARE THE SAME HEART.

*Then Moses went to Mount Nebo from the plains of Moab and climbed Pisgah Peak, which is across from Jericho. And the LORD showed him the whole land, from Gilead as far as Dan; all the land of Naphtali; the land of Ephraim and Manasseh; all the land of Judah, extending to the Mediterranean Sea; the Negev, the Jordan Valley with Jericho—the city of palms—as far as Zoar. Then the LORD said to Moses, "This is the land I promised on oath to Abraham, Isaac, and Jacob, and I told them I would give it to their descendants. I have now allowed you to see it, but you will not enter the land." So Moses, the servant of the LORD, died there in the land of Moab, just as the LORD had said. *The LORD buried him in a valley near Beth-peor in Moab, but to this day no one knows the exact place. (Deuteronomy 34:1-6, NLT) *Hebrew*

There was no hint of withdrawn love from God toward the person of Moses. In His graciousness, God showed his friend the land of promise from the top of a high peak and then lovingly buried him with dignity and care.

Nearing Moses' death, *"...the Lord commissioned Joshua son of Nun with these words: 'Be strong and courageous! You must bring the people of Israel into the land I swore to give them. I will be with you'"* (Deuteronomy 31:23, NLT). There are those beautiful words again... *"I will be with you."* Just as God had dispelled all of Moses' fear and excuses, He assured Joshua His presence would be enough. *"Now Joshua son of Nun was full of the spirit of wisdom, for Moses had laid his hands on him. So the people of Israel obeyed him and did everything just as the LORD had commanded Moses"* (Deuteronomy 34:9, NLT). Moses was dead, the transition was complete, and it was time for Joshua to lead.

God wasted no time giving Joshua instructions to move ahead. He said,

> *Now that my servant Moses is dead, you must lead my people across the Jordan River into the land I am giving them. I promise you what I promised Moses: "Everywhere you go, you will be on land I have given you—from the Negev Desert in the south to the Lebanon mountains in the north, from the Euphrates River on the east to the Mediterranean Sea on the west, and all the land of the Hittites." No one will be able to stand their ground against you as long as you live. For I will be with you as I was with Moses. I will not fail or abandon you. Be strong and courageous, for you will lead*

my people to possess all the land I swore to give their ancestors. Be strong and very courageous. Obey all the laws Moses gave you. Do not turn away from them, and you will be successful in everything you do. Study this Book of the Law continually. Meditate on it day and night so you may be sure to obey all that is written in it. Only then will you succeed. I command you—be strong and courageous! Do not be afraid or discouraged. For the LORD your God is with you wherever you go. (Joshua 1:2-9, NLT)

God's guarantee of His presence bolstered Joshua's resolve in walking out the promises given him. Notice God's two commands: *Be strong and courageous* and *Study the Book of the Law continually*. God made it very clear to Joshua that he had no room in his life for fear and discouragement. When we are about God's business and filled with His presence, there's no room left for fear and discouragement. When we give place to these emotions and allow them to take root in our hearts, we're unseating His purpose and presence. It's a daily choice. That's why God repeated Himself three times in this passage alone—*Be strong and courageous!*

WHEN WE ARE ABOUT GOD'S BUSINESS AND FILLED WITH HIS PRESENCE, THERE'S NO ROOM LEFT FOR FEAR AND DISCOURAGEMENT.

God's second command given here, *Study the Book of the Law continually*, isn't a casual suggestion. Notice the outcome connected to the directive—*Only then will you succeed.* Oh, how I long for the Body of Christ to see the critical link between saturating ourselves with

God's Word and success! We have traded *His* success for a knock-off offered by the world. We don't even realize what we *could* have because we've not identified and internalized His words to us. As Christians, we should outshine those around us who don't name Christ as Lord. Michael Pitts, in his book *Power Shifters,* said, "Christians should be the sharpest thinkers, the hardest workers, the best writers, the most creative artists, the most trustworthy employees, the most principled businesspeople, and the most skilled professionals of any in society." This is part of God's definition of success for us, not just because it makes us attractive, but because it exalts His name when His kids are intimately tapped into His source of power and creativity. None of this is possible without an absolute saturation of His Word and appropriation of His principles in our lives.

But, I don't see the Christian community taking this seriously. Perhaps we're adjusting God's instructions to fit our desires and expectations. Hmmm...maybe we need to go back and reread the first half of this chapter—pretty serious business.

As we consider painful transitions in our own lives, our surest method of remaining steady through the change is to lean into the only One who knows the end from the beginning and loves us perfectly. In making major personal shifts, we may experience death in some form or fashion, whether it's the actual death of someone we're intimately connected to or the death of a dream or expectation (my book, *In the Stillness,* addresses this in detail). But, the beauty of God is that even in the loss, there is life in the One who never gives up on us and finishes every good work He began in us as we trust His leading.

Transitions can be long, and many people give up the fight to overcome due to their lack of endurance. Because we aren't able to control timing, detours, roadblocks, and outcomes, we must find our contentment in our relationship with Christ. The long days and nights of waiting become a beautiful breeding ground for joy and trust in our Savior, knowing that our ultimate goal is a friendship with Him that is carried into eternity. That's what Moses focused on. I'm sure he experienced disappointment over not stepping into the Promised Land after all those years of faithful service, but his friendship with God trumped this world's unfulfilled expectations and ushered him into eternity with his best friend.

THE LONG DAYS AND NIGHTS OF WAITING BECOME A BEAUTIFUL BREEDING GROUND FOR JOY AND TRUST IN OUR SAVIOR.

And, in contrast, Joshua's most productive and challenging years were just getting started. As one fades, another rises. This is how we were designed to transition, and gracefully walking through the paces of change brings God's name honor. I have watched graceful changes and also had a front row seat to very unattractive transition. God's honor through his children is at stake in the way we handle these changes. Clawing and clinging to position instead of gracefully releasing is, at its root, childishly self-focused. Marking territory does not make room for the promotion of others. As we keep our eyes on our Savior and listen intently for the Holy Spirit's leading, we'll know when to open our hand to make room for God's next leaders. If needed, God will pry our hands loose, but why not trust His timing and know that He has good plans for us as we transition out of one season and into the next. Kingdom-mindedness releases us from holding too tightly to that which belongs to Him anyway. Let go; it'll be all right!

CHAPTER SIX

One Last Push

DURING TRANSITION, GOD HOLDS us in a balancing act of what has been and what will be, preparing our hearts and positioning players for all that is yet to come. Healing past wounds and strengthening faltering faith are part of the transitional period. Allowing God to mold and use us activates our cooperation with His timeline, and it is always somewhat different than our own expectations. We don't realize what avenues of our thinking need to be transformed or realigned. This is important work, and we would do well to lean into His processes in us and be patient through this period of transformation. As transition nears completion, we often experience one last push that definitively closes the door on the past and releases all holds on our next season.

HEALING PAST WOUNDS AND STRENGTHENING FALTERING FAITH ARE PART OF THE TRANSITIONAL PERIOD.

In the book of Joshua, chapters one through five record Joshua's last push between Moses' death and conquering the Promised Land. Joshua told the people to ready themselves. *"In three days you will cross the Jordan River and take possession of the land the LORD your God has given you"* (Joshua 1:11, NLT). He then secretly sent two spies into the land, focusing on Jericho as their first battle site. He had personally experienced the disastrous results from the first spying expedition and was determined not to give the people the chance to speak doubt into the situation the second time around.

The expedition yielded a favorable report, and Joshua led the people to the banks of the Jordan River. With the Ark of the Covenant in front of the people, the priests stepped into the river, and just as the Red Sea was transformed into a dry path, the Jordan yielded its waters to God's children. Joshua's time had come. *"That day the LORD made Joshua great in the eyes of all the Israelites, and for the rest of his life they revered him as much as they had revered Moses"* (Joshua 4:14, NLT). Just as God's stamp of approval had been on Moses' life, His hand was on Joshua.

With Joshua at the helm, entering the Promised Land meant taking possession of the land. There would be many battles yet ahead. God proceeded to do three things before sending the people into battle: memorialize the threshold; consecrate the people; and cut off the provision of their past. Their new day had come, and it was time to set their eyes toward their future.

A memorial is intended to be a constant reminder of a red-letter day, event, or person. In this case, God instructed Joshua to construct a memorial of the day God's presence led the Israelites across the Jordan River. While crossing the Jordan, He told Joshua,

Now choose twelve men, one from each tribe. Tell the men to take twelve stones from where the priests are standing in the middle of the Jordan and pile them up at the place where you camp tonight... It was there at Gilgal that Joshua piled up the twelve stones taken from the Jordan River. Then Joshua said to the Israelites, "In the future, your children will ask, 'What do these stones mean?' Then you can tell them, 'This is where the Israelites crossed the Jordan on dry ground.' For the LORD your God dried up the river right before your eyes, and he kept it dry until you were all across, just as he did at the Red Sea when he dried it up until we had all crossed over. He did this so that all the nations of the earth might know the power of the LORD, and that you might fear the LORD your God forever." (Joshua 4:2-3, 20-24, NLT).

GOD WILL OFTEN MARK PERIODS OF TRANSITIONS WITH MEMORABLE EVENTS OR THRESHOLDS.

They were crossing into new territory with a new leader. God marked this transition in the lives of His children with a miracle and a memorial. Forever, this day would be remembered. Forever, His children would be different. In the eyes of the surrounding nations, these people of God were now feared, a force too strong to overcome. The Israelites were being shifted from a position of weakness to a position of strength by God Himself. The twelve stones laid upon one another became a memorial to this threshold that had been crossed. In our lives as well, God will often mark periods of transitions with memorable events or thresholds. Sometimes it's the death of one close to us that launches us with a new life trajectory. A job loss can become a definitive moment that frees us to pursue what's been in our hearts for so long. When the last child leaves home, we may find ourselves dedicating our future to a new direction at God's bidding. These transitions often wound and change us at the same time. God strategically plans our life seasons, and with cooperation on our part, we can stay in step with what God is doing.

However, because of our stubborn human nature, just declaring that today is the first day of the rest of our lives doesn't necessarily have enough buy-in power. Commitment requires skin in the game. Once we have suffered for a cause, we're much more likely to see it through to completion. The memorial built with the twelve stones served as a beautiful reminder of their river-crossing miracle, but God's children needed a little something more to solidify their resolve for the coming battles. *"At that time, the LORD told Joshua, 'Use knives of flint to make the Israelites a circumcised people again.' So Joshua made flint knives and circumcised the entire male population of Israel at Gibeath-haaraloth"* (Joshua 5:2-3, NLT).

COMMITMENT REQUIRES SKIN IN THE GAME.

These resistant generations had been through much since the days of Abraham when the covenant of circumcision was first introduced. It was time to return to the original call to be set apart as God's covenant people. No new thing in our lives initiated by God can proceed without consecration. There would be people groups to conquer in the new land, many of which would have undue influence on the Israelites. Their commitment to being God's children had to be firm. Taking new ground always positions us to interact with that which has the potential to move us away from God. And, God was going to great lengths to cause His children to draw near to Him. The covenant served as a reminder that all the people had to do was obey, and God would do the rest. As we draw near to His presence, our hearts have a greater tendency to desire obedience toward Him. So, God was beckoning His children in a rather painful way to set themselves apart and declare their loyalty once again. Although we normally see pain as undesirable, it usually serves as a good reminder.

> NO NEW THING IN OUR LIVES INITIATED BY GOD CAN PROCEED WITHOUT CONSECRATION.

The circumcised males rested in the camp until they were healed. *"Then the LORD said to Joshua, 'Today I have rolled away the shame of your slavery in Egypt'"* (Joshua 5:9, NLT). The slavery of yesterday was gone, and the victory of today became their new identity. It's interesting that forty years earlier, God provided measures for implementing this very freedom, but the people wouldn't accept them. They chose, instead, to live in their slavery mentality. God had to replace that generation because they just couldn't make the transition. Just like those Israelites, there are people today who cannot go forward into the victory God has planned for tomorrow because they aren't willing to make a break from their past. Reaching for God's promises just seems like too much of a risk. It's a trust issue. That first generation didn't trust

God. Now, this new generation was ready, and God could move His plans forward.

Before heading into battle, there was one last tie to the past to sever—the provision of yesterday.

While the Israelites were camped at Gilgal on the plains of Jericho, they celebrated Passover on the evening of the fourteenth day of the first month—the month that marked their exodus from Egypt. The very next day they began to eat unleavened bread and roasted grain harvested from the land. No manna appeared that day, and it was never seen again. So from that time on the Israelites ate from the crops of Canaan. (Joshua 5:10-12, NLT). Manna had represented their provision during their years of wandering and waiting for God's promise to be fulfilled. The provision of manna wasn't meant to be their sustenance forever; rather, it was a temporary measure God used to take care of His children.

THERE ARE PEOPLE TODAY WHO CANNOT GO FORWARD INTO THE VICTORY GOD HAS PLANNED FOR TOMORROW BECAUSE THEY AREN'T WILLING TO MAKE A BREAK FROM THEIR PAST.

God uses temporary measures for us as well during times of transition. These periods of time can get long, and sometimes we get so used to the temporary provision that we begin thinking this is God's intended will for our future. During transition, God miraculously handed His children their daily provision. Now, in their land of harvest, God removed His daily hand-out, requiring them to fully live in the blessing of their fulfillment. Without realizing it, we can become dependent on God's hand-outs, and when it comes time for us to live in the fulfillment of our promise, we struggle to see ourselves as anything more than manna-eaters. God is telling us to go forth and conquer, and we retreat to our spoon-fed dependence.

How we perceive ourselves during transition will show up when we're released into our blessing. The transition is a temporary dwelling place. The people knew during their wilderness trek that they were waiting for the unfaithful generation to die so they could take hold of their promise. This new generation needed to see themselves as conquerors-in-waiting. If they didn't keep that mindset during the transition, they wouldn't be able to step into their destiny when God said, "Go!" It's incredibly sad to watch people power down during a long transition and simply accept their manna-eating position as their lot in life. Don't give up the promise just because it's taking longer than you thought it would to see the fulfillment! Stay focused on God and His Word no matter how long it takes. A prayer I have continuously prayed over the last few years of transition has been, "Lord, keep my eyes fixed on Your Holy Spirit. May I sense Your movement and stay in step with You so I don't miss any opportunity You have for me." Although outward appearances indicated nothing significant was happening in my world, I never stopped anticipating what was heading my direction. My manna-eating days were coming to a close, and I wanted to be ready to step into His promise.

HOW WE PERCEIVE OURSELVES DURING TRANSITION WILL SHOW UP WHEN WE'RE RELEASED INTO OUR BLESSING.

The very day the Israelites ate the harvest of their land of promise, the provision of the past was removed. I think the question begs to be asked, "What is God transitioning in my life that requires me to let go of the provision of the past?" This provision could be material, but it could also be relational, emotional, or spiritual. Paul, in his letter to the Philippians, said, *"...I am focusing all my energies on this one thing: Forgetting the past and looking forward to what lies ahead"* (Philippians, 3:13, NLT). When we see ourselves as conquerors and co-laborers with Christ, we can move forward with authority to accomplish His purposes. If we hold onto what has propped us up in the past, our vision is focused the wrong direction, and our forward movement is curtailed. Draw a line in the sand of your life, and let go of your manna-eating days! God is on the move, and He's calling us to stay in step with Him.

WHEN WE SEE OURSELVES AS CONQUERORS AND CO-LABORERS WITH CHRIST, WE CAN MOVE FORWARD WITH AUTHORITY TO ACCOMPLISH HIS PURPOSES.

CHAPTER SEVEN

Entering In

UNDER JOSHUA'S LEADERSHIP, God's children were ready to take possession of the land. Laying hold of God's promises never comes without a fight. But, in keeping with God's majesty and power, He assures us that the fight really belongs to Him, and all we have to do is walk in cooperation with Him. God's instructions to Joshua for conquering Jericho came with clarity and definitive authority.

> LAYING HOLD OF GOD'S PROMISES NEVER COMES WITHOUT A FIGHT.

But the LORD said to Joshua, "I have given you Jericho, its king, and all its mighty warriors. Your entire army is to march around the city once a day for six days. Seven priests will walk ahead of the Ark, each carrying a ram's horn. On the seventh day you are to march around the city seven times, with the priests blowing the horns. When you hear the priests give one long blast on the horns, have all the people give a mighty shout. Then the walls of the city will collapse, and the people can charge straight into the city." (Joshua 6:2-5, NLT)

The people did as they were told, and the city of Jericho fell. However, the victory was not as clean-cut as it appeared. There is an interesting verse hidden in the second chapter of First Chronicles. Amid a long genealogical list of names, verse seven reads, *"The son of Carmi was Achan, the troubler of Israel, who transgressed in the accursed thing."* Before delving into the meaning of this verse, let's explore the back-story of Achan and how it relates to the "entering in" of God's people.

Just before God flattened the city of Jericho on behalf of His children, Joshua gave the Israelites specific instructions from the Lord. He commanded,

> *"The city and everything in it must be completely destroyed as an offering to the Lord. Only Rahab the prostitute and the others in her house will be spared, for she protected our spies. Do not take any of the things set apart for destruction, or you yourselves will be completely destroyed, and you will bring trouble on all Israel. Everything made from silver, gold, bronze, or iron is sacred to the Lord and must be brought into his treasury." (Joshua 6:17-19, NLT)*

Upon their victorious defeat of Jericho, the Israelites and Joshua became famous throughout the land. A city called Ai became the next target, and this seemed like easy prey. About three thousand men marched confidently on the city. Oddly enough, the Israelites were soundly defeated, and they turned tail and ran. In their retreat, thirty-six men were killed, and they were now the laughing stock of the surrounding people groups. Joshua and the leaders of Israel fell on their faces before

God, beseeching Him for explanation. God promptly told them to get up. The reason they had been defeated was simple; He was angry with them. Someone had taken some of the banned items from Jericho and had hidden them in his tent. The punishment was clearly stated, *"The one who has stolen what was set apart for destruction will himself be burned with fire, along with everything he has, for he has broken the covenant of the Lord and has done a horrible thing in Israel"* (Joshua 7:15, NLT). God singled out the guilty man; Achan and his family were stoned to death, and their bodies burned. God told Joshua to take another run at Ai, and this time He would go before them. Ai was soundly defeated.

SIN IS NEVER KEPT IN ISOLATION.

Now, let's look again at the verse from First Chronicles, *"The son of Carmi was Achan, the troubler of Israel, who transgressed in the accursed thing."* We certainly see why Achan was called "the troubler of Israel," and we'll touch more on this in a minute. But, what about the words, *"who transgressed in the accursed thing?"* Another way of phrasing that could be, "who withheld *for himself* those things set apart as holy unto God." God had given the people specific instructions through Joshua. They were not to take anything for themselves.

Achan, we assume, never meant to cause harm to his family or his fellow Israelites. He simply saw something he wanted, coveted it, quietly took it, and hid it. But, sin is never kept in isolation. We would like to believe we can choose to sin and keep it between ourselves and God, but that isn't possible. Even if it's not right away, our sin will eventually produce a landslide of side-effects. In Achan's case, his decision cost thirty-six soldiers' lives, a smeared name for Israel, his own life, and the lives of his family.

You may be thinking, "Thank goodness that I don't have any outright sin like Achan," but let's go a little deeper. *What have you kept for yourself that belongs to the Lord?* I encourage you to pause, read that question again, and then wait on the Lord for a few minutes.

Whether we like it or not, our lives tend to be a reflection of our selfishness. By (sin) nature, we want to keep our money, our time, our families, our talents, and our possessions to ourselves. None of these things were meant to be kept; they were meant to be given away, sown into the lives of others for the growth of the Kingdom of God.

WHETHER WE LIKE IT OR NOT, OUR LIVES TEND TO BE A REFLECTION OF OUR SELFISHNESS.

How we handle our money is probably the best indicator of the position of our hearts. Paul warns in 1 Timothy 6:9-10 (NLT), *"But people who long to be rich fall into temptation and are trapped by many foolish and harmful desires that plunge them into ruin and destruction. For the love of money is at the root of all kinds of evil. And some people, craving money, have wandered from the faith and pierced themselves with many sorrows."* When our desire to make money for the sake of having more overtakes our desire to use our resources for the Kingdom, we've established an idol. It's easy to let our focus slide in the wrong direction. We must keep our purpose in the Kingdom of God at the forefront. If that purpose rules our decision-making process, then we can rest assured that our priorities will stay in line. *"He will give you all you need from day to day if you live for Him and make the Kingdom of God your primary concern"* (Matthew 6:33, NLT).

Time is right up there next to money as an indicator of the position of our hearts. God may be tugging on your heart to use your time differently than you've been operating lately. It's really about having our priorities straight and placing the needs of the Kingdom above our own. We often err in using our time to put out fires, so to speak, instead of investing our time in the lives of others, including our families. There will always be situations shouting for your immediate attention, but the quiet longings of your family's hearts will go unmet if you're not intentional about your time. No one else is able to invest in your family as you can.

THE QUIET LONGINGS OF YOUR FAMILY'S HEARTS WILL GO UNMET IF YOU'RE NOT INTENTIONAL ABOUT YOUR TIME.

Admittedly, it's easy to allow our children to simply grow up in our homes without truly pouring ourselves into them. Our goal is to mentor these selfish little rascals into adulthood with Christ-like character, Kingdom purpose, and dream-inspired vision. That doesn't happen without incredible intentionality and a lot of time invested. The Bible says that children are like arrows in the hands of a warrior (Psalm 127). Warriors have purpose, and they craft their arrows to fly long and straight to hit a bulls-eye. It's our job as parents to ask God for vision into our children's tomorrow and then creatively pursue paths to lead them there. And, then, when they are grown, we must release them purposefully. Your children are not yours to keep. God has entrusted them to you for a short time with the purpose of preparing them to take their place in His Kingdom. Please don't keep for yourself that which has been set apart for His use. You've prepared your children to fly. Now, pull the string on your bow taut and shoot them straight and true into His purpose for them.

YOU'VE PREPARED YOUR CHILDREN TO FLY. NOW, PULL THE STRING ON YOUR BOW TAUT AND SHOOT THEM STRAIGHT AND TRUE INTO HIS PURPOSE FOR THEM.

Equally important is sowing our talents into the Kingdom. We mustn't get so caught up in the daily routine that we let our talents sit on the shelf. When we do, we're robbing ourselves of fulfillment and the Kingdom of God of our purpose. Using what God has placed in us involves risk. He may call us, like Joshua, into new territory. If we shrink back, we're playing it safe and not giving to God what has been set apart for His use. I wish I could tell you that it's your decision—to boldly risk or choose to play it safe. But, this isn't the stock market, and you don't own your investment. Your life has been purchased by the blood of Christ and is to be set apart for Him alone.

All we are and all we have is to be His and used as He chooses. Nothing we have will go with us into eternity, but somehow we've attached ourselves to our belongings as if we're taking them with us. We need to hold our possessions with an open hand. It becomes a trust issue. We tend to let go of only that which we believe will come back to us if needed. God knows what we need and when we need it. If He asks us to let go of what we have, it's for the purpose of blessing others and teaching us to trust His provision for our tomorrow. If this is an area of difficulty for you, ask Him to take you on a journey to master this. He is kind, and as you desire to learn the art of keeping an open hand, He will be pleased to teach you. You will be amazed at what will flow in and out of your hands as you allow Him to use your life. The moment we close our hand out of fear of lack, we cut off His generous provision.

GOD DESIRES THAT WE TRUST HIM ENOUGH WITH OUR WOUNDED HEARTS THAT WE WILL OFFER OUR PAIN TO HIM IN AN ACT OF HUMILITY.

Likewise, when we have been through painful circumstances, we have a tendency to become closed-fisted in matters of the heart. Attempting to minimize future pain by closing off what's been wounded is a natural reaction. The problem is that we also close off our relationship to the only One who can truly help us heal. We call it protection. God calls it sin. Releasing the grip on our hearts brings vulnerability that many wounded people simply cannot embrace. But, with this unselfish act of vulnerability comes the beauty of worship and loving others. God desires that we trust Him enough with our wounded hearts that we will offer our pain to Him in an act of humility. He's gentle and kind. If we keep our grip tight around our hearts, the pain turns to bitterness, and we shut God out, leaving us unable to receive or give love. Life becomes existence, and our purpose is lost in our pain.

Anything we keep for ourselves (money, time, children, talents, possessions, or our hearts) that God has set apart for Himself is sin and will cause friction. If we don't quickly fix the problem, we will bring damage to our families and our community. If we'll keep in mind that this life is truly not about us, we will have a much better shot at hitting the correct target with our lives. Achan will be forever known as *the troubler*. That's not the by-line we would like to have engraved on our tombstones. Be a giver of all you are and have rather than a person who keeps and hides for himself.

As we enter into God's plan and purpose, *how* we enter becomes crucial. Will we be like Achan, hesitant to obey and withholding in our attitude? Or, will we walk forward with complete abandon and unquestioning trust? *How* we enter determines our victory or defeat in taking possession of all that God has promised. Trust Him!

CHAPTER EIGHT

On the Battlefront

WITH VALUABLE LESSONS LEARNED at Jericho and Ai, Joshua and the Israelites moved forward in their conquest of the Promised Land. There was ground to be taken, and Joshua was careful to obey the LORD's commands left by Moses. From Joshua's battlefront experiences, three major lessons emerge: 1)You are more easily deceived than you think you are; 2)Don't leave anything standing that God said kill; and 3)Be prepared for the battle to take longer than you think it will.

Because of Joshua's fame, all the kings west of the Jordan feared the people of Israel. Most of these kings combined their armies to make war against the Israelites. *"But when the people of Gibeon heard what had happened to Jericho and Ai, they resorted to deception to save themselves"* (Joshua 9:3-4, NLT). These Gibeonites portrayed themselves as travelers from a distant land, seeking peace with Joshua. Instructions had been given by God not to make peace treaties with the inhabitants of Canaan (which these people actually were). Their convincing evidence said otherwise, causing Joshua and the Israelite leaders to believe their deceptive story. Even the words the Gibeonites spoke sounded reasonable,

> *This bread was hot from the ovens when we left. But now, as you can see, it is dry and moldy. These wineskins were new when we filled them, but now they are old and cracked. And our clothing and sandals are worn out from our long, hard trip. (Joshua 9:12-13, NLT)*

But, it's the next verse that is indicting. *"So the Israelite leaders examined their bread, but they did not consult the LORD"* (v.14). Joshua was committed to seeking the LORD before going into physical battle. However, this deceptive encounter with the Gibeonites slid in undetected. Israel's leaders certainly didn't expect to be lied to and relied on their own reasoning to make a decision. They examined the evidence and allowed it to dictate their actions. *"Then Joshua went ahead and signed a peace treaty with them, and the leaders of Israel ratified their agreement with a binding oath. Three days later, the facts came out..."* (Joshua 9:15-16, NLT).

WE COME TO CONCLUSIONS ABOUT PEOPLE AND SITUATIONS BASED ON FAULTY EVIDENCE.

Instead of consulting the Lord, they relied on their instincts, ultimately basing their conclusions on lies. We do this in *our* lives as well if we're not careful. We come to conclusions about people and situations based on faulty evidence. Have you ever assigned a label to someone based on the words of a third party? Perhaps those words were false evidence, and your conclusion about them is wrong. What about events, programs, or ministries to which you assigned negative motivation? Without speaking to the initiator, you can't know the person's true motivation. In the Body of Christ, we have a tendency to do enormous damage to one another by examining each other with our own reasoning and developing wrong conclusions based on false evidence. The way to combat this is to consult the Lord! When we go before the Father truly wanting to see things from His perspective, He will help us see with clarity any area that directly affects us, and He often tells us to simply walk in love with those we need to stop examining. As we walk in reliance on the leading of the Holy Spirit, He purifies our motives. He warns us of danger or deception as we lean into Him, and we must be careful not to assign faulty conclusions based on false evidence. Simply keeping our eyes on Him is always our best course of action.

AS WE WALK IN RELIANCE ON THE LEADING OF THE HOLY SPIRIT, HE PURIFIES OUR MOTIVES.

The second lesson I mentioned from Joshua's days on the battlefront is not to leave standing anything God said kill. When we contemplate the person of Joshua, we usually assign all the positive leader-like qualities that make us admire him so much. But, there was a side to Joshua that might make us a little uncomfortable. When it came to carrying out the battle campaign the Lord gave him, he wasn't a nice guy! Through Moses, God had made Joshua's parameters clear; he was to kill every person in the towns they attacked.

> *So, Joshua conquered the whole region—the kings and the people of the hill country, the Negev, the western foothills, and the mountain slopes. He completely*

destroyed everyone in the land, leaving no survivors, just as the LORD, the God of Israel, had commanded. Joshua slaughtered them from Kadesh-barnea to Gaza and from Goshen to Gibeon. In a single campaign Joshua conquered all these kings and their land, for the LORD, the God of Israel, was fighting for his people. (Joshua 10:40-42, NLT)

Although walking in kindness is how we, as Christians, are to operate, there are critical moments when God expects us to kill that which He says needs to die in our lives. We may have allowed a relationship to linger that needs to be cut off. Attitudes that God has actively and persistently pointed out in our hearts we've allowed to remain. Fears that must be confronted we've buried at the bottom of our to-do list. These undealt-with battles will always resurface as hindrances in our future. We must not leave standing what God says to kill. *"And Joshua did as he was told, carefully obeying all of the LORD's instructions to Moses* (Joshua 11:15, NLT). Will we make the hard choices when God expects us to?

THERE ARE CRITICAL MOMENTS WHEN GOD EXPECTS US TO KILL THAT WHICH HE SAYS NEEDS TO DIE IN OUR LIVES.

In the midst of the battles God asks us to face, our resolve is often tested by the length of time we must endure. That brings us to our third lesson; be prepared for the battle to take longer than you think it will. As we read of Joshua's conquests, we're able to take in all the battles from the first to the last within six short chapters, but in reality, these confrontations took several years. Joshua 11:18 says that Joshua killed all the kings of that area, "*waging war for a long time to accomplish this*" (NLT). Those are not welcomed words to us. Persisting in something that's difficult and drawn out requires strength to endure.

Our battlefield often feels like a prison holding us back from the freedom we so desperately seek. However, the long view yields an amazing outcome; our prison was actually the breeding ground for our victory. If our battles were short-lived, we would have no reason to confront the self-sabotaging tendencies in our lives. The longer the battle, the more deeply we examine our attitudes, actions, and motivations. If we'll allow the prison time to be our field of change, we'll emerge victorious in ways we couldn't have imagined. The growth potential in prison experiences is unobtainable any other way. Your prison may be an unexpected diagnosis, a financial crisis, a devastated relationship, or a personal failure. If you choose to sit in the corner of your prison cell and sulk, your time will be wasted. If, instead, you use this time to self-examine, seek the Lord, and determine to walk forward, your victory will be sweet.

THE LONG VIEW YIELDS AN AMAZING OUTCOME; OUR PRISON WAS ACTUALLY THE BREEDING GROUND FOR OUR VICTORY.

It seems obvious which choice is better; one is damaging, and one is productive. However, it's rather amazing how many people choose to waste their prison opportunity. I doubt it's because they can't see the possibility, but rather because their endurance hasn't been trained to withstand the length of time. Abandonment of self doesn't come until we embrace the realization that we can't control the outcome. We find ourselves kicking against the process that is trying to change us. We want to control timing and circumstances, but the very essence of permanent character change in our lives comes from the total relinquishing of control. It's counterintuitive to give up control when our lives desperately need reordering.

We often feel as if we're losing time in prison, that opportunities are passing us by. But, in fact, the character changes that are being wrought in us during our confinement will be what hold us steady in the days of victory yet ahead. (We'll delve into the test of success in the next chapter.) So, the time we feel hedged in is not the time to try to break free. Give in to the process, and let the internal work have its way. This is truly a position of humility before the Lord. Everything in us wants to fight, and God says, "*Be still.*"

> ABANDONMENT OF SELF DOESN'T COME UNTIL WE EMBRACE THE REALIZATION THAT WE CAN'T CONTROL THE OUTCOME.

In that stillness, He'll show us the long view of our captivity. We'll begin to see what He's trying to accomplish in us, and we then realize the importance of our cooperation. I'm in year six of a personal prison sentence, and what God has done in me during these years of confinement is nothing short of miraculous. I fought against the process for the first year, begged to be released for the next two, and finally gave up all resistance by year four. In the last two years, God has significantly extended my field of influence, poured words into me for the publishing of six books, and opened doors to preach. When I finally gave in to the process, God was unhindered to accomplish His purposes.

We often don't realize how strong we've grown during our confinement, but others looking on do. Although the event that landed us in prison started out as a curse word to us, we learn to see it as a blessing. The day my world came to a crashing halt six years ago had no indication of being a landmark day. In my pain, I put on my running shoes and took off out the front door. Today, I run half-marathons and compete in triathlons. My oldest daughter has joined me, and what started in desperation has become a beautiful blessing and source of joy in my life. My physical body is stronger now than six years ago.

My desperation also drove me to my knees spiritually. Although my relationship with God was good to begin with, I have now found a place in Him of such satisfaction, love, and peace that I can honestly say I am grateful for the painful events that landed me in my prison. Relationally, because of my hedged-in place, I have discovered the necessity of deep personal friendships. Today, I am surrounded by authentic relationships that fuel my life and enrich my dreams. Am I better off today than the day of my imprisonment? Absolutely! My freedom is at hand, and the strength that has been developed in my life during my prison years is propelling me toward the fulfillment of God's plans. Embrace the depth of change God is implementing in your life. I can't promise

> ALTHOUGH THE EVENT THAT LANDED US IN PRISON STARTED OUT AS A CURSE WORD TO US, WE LEARN TO SEE IT AS A BLESSING.

your sentence will be shortened by your cooperation, but I *can* promise that your emergent strength will be great. Don't give up, but definitely give in!

CHAPTER NINE

The Real Test

As we dive into this chapter, it's necessary that we see the Israelites' position in full color near the end of Joshua's life. So, I will include the whole of chapter twenty-three from the book of Joshua. Please don't just skim over the words, but actually take in every verse; each one bears weight on the concluding two chapters of this book.

> *The years passed, and the LORD had given the people of Israel rest from all their enemies. Joshua, who was now very old, called together all the elders, leaders, judges, and officers of Israel. He said to them, "I am an old man now. You have seen everything the LORD your God has done for you during my lifetime. The LORD your God has fought for you against your enemies. I have allotted to you as an inheritance all the land of the nations yet unconquered, as well as the land of those we have already conquered—from the Jordan River to the Mediterranean Sea in the west. This land will be yours, for the LORD your God will drive out all the people living there now. You will live there instead of them, just as the LORD your God promised you. So be strong! Be*

very careful to follow all the instructions written in the Book of the Law of Moses. Do not deviate from them in any way. Make sure you do not associate with the other people still remaining in the land. Do not even mention the names of their gods, much less swear by them or worship them. But be faithful to the LORD your God as you have done until now. For the LORD has driven out great and powerful nations for you, and no one has yet been able to defeat you. Each one of you will put to flight a thousand of the enemy, for the LORD your God fights for you, just as he has promised. So be very careful to love the LORD your God. But if you turn away from him and intermarry with the survivors of these nations remaining among you, then know for certain that the LORD your God will no longer drive them out from your land. Instead, they will be a snare and a trap for you, a pain in your side and a thorn in your eyes, and you will be wiped out from this good land the LORD your God has given you. Soon I will die, going the way of all the earth. Deep in your hearts you know that every promise of the LORD your God has come true. Not a single one has failed! But as surely as the LORD your God has given you the good things he promised, he will also bring disaster on you if you disobey him. He will completely wipe you out from this good land he has given you. If you break the covenant of the LORD your God by worshiping and serving other gods, his anger will burn against you, and you will quickly be wiped out from the good land he has given you." (NLT)

Joshua's leadership provided the people with a structure of obedience and passionate pursuit of all that God had promised them. This generation seemed to get it; they took hold of Joshua's heartbeat and made it their own. *"And the Israelites served the LORD throughout the lifetime of Joshua and the leaders who outlived him—those who had seen all the great things the LORD had done for Israel"* (Judges 2:7, NLT). This sounds like a beautiful recipe for success! God had established Himself as Israel's Hero, and the people entered into covenant to worship Him alone. But, apparently, the people weren't diligent in raising up the next generation to love and revere the God to whom they had faithfully committed themselves. Three verses later, we read, *"After that generation died, another generation grew up who did not acknowledge the LORD or remember the mighty things he had done for Israel. Then the Israelites did what was evil in the LORD's sight and worshiped the images of Baal"* (Judges 2:10-11, NLT).

I don't know about you, but there's something about those verses that makes me want to pack it up and go home. No matter how much the Lord did for them, they kept doing their own thing. Human nature is maddening both in us *and* others! However, if we examine what went wrong, we can learn some valuable lessons to apply in our own lives. The unconquered land mentioned in chapter twenty-three stood as the real test of Israel's beliefs and resolve. God had been so faithful to set them up for success; He proved His mighty power, gave them exceptional leadership, and promised He would help them be victorious in the battles yet ahead. But, apparently this new generation didn't believe Him. They are indicted for not acknowledging God and not remembering what He had done for Israel.

As the Israelites approached these unconquered lands, they were expected to be strong and courageous, knowing that God would be with them, providing them with victory in every battle. But, Judges (chapter one) reveals that the majority of the tribes failed to drive the Canaanites from their land, the very land God had said was theirs to possess. Why? Perhaps three reasons will help us understand what went so terribly wrong.

First, with the leadership of Joshua gone, their unified purpose lost momentum. Did Joshua neglect to raise up a leader to take his place, or did he expect that the people would actually adhere to and remain under God's leadership even into the next generation? Perhaps both. With the shift in authority from Joshua to the tribal leaders, the people lost their focus. Leadership change is sometimes precarious and always requires intentional strategy. Joshua reminded the people of God's promises and their own blind spots. They had a great tendency (like us) to believe that they could stand above their temptations rather than building protective barriers. When there is a gap in leadership, people tend to resort to doing their own thing.

LEADERSHIP CHANGE IS SOMETIMES PRECARIOUS AND ALWAYS REQUIRES INTENTIONAL STRATEGY.

A second contributor to Israel's spiral downward was the length of time it took to complete the conquest. We discussed endurance in the last chapter, and we have a great tendency to underestimate its influence on us. This conquest spanned many years (into subsequent generations), and the people grew weary of fighting. They seemed to lose their intensity and wavered in their belief that God was the victorious factor. It takes great discipline to stay focused on a goal over a long period of time.

Third, the people saw the enemy's strength as invincible. *"The LORD was with the people of Judah, and they took possession of the hill country. But they failed to drive out the people living in the plains because the people there had iron chariots"* (Judges 1:19, NLT). I don't remember God saying anything to the Israelites about excusing opponents with iron chariots. God clearly had told His children that He would help them and that they were to conquer *all* the inhabitants of the land. There were no exceptions, but the people shrank back in fear. What they left undealt with became their downfall. Those people groups the Israelites let live worshiped idols that eventually led God's children astray. Instead of obeying God's instructions, they changed them to suit their situation. They didn't follow through on what God had said.

IT TAKES GREAT DISCIPLINE TO STAY FOCUSED ON A GOAL OVER A LONG PERIOD OF TIME.

When our lives need rescuing, we intensely pray and give God wide berth in our lives to be our Hero. But, the real test comes after He stills the raging storm on our behalf. Will we, in gratitude, stay intense and focused about pursuing Him and His ways, or will we get comfortable and go back to doing things with the same attitude that set us up to fail the first time? I see Christians make this fatal mistake all the time. They act as if they've forgotten what God has done for them (just like the Israelites), and they go back to their original mode of operation—until the next crisis arises. God is incredibly gracious, but at some point He will excuse Himself from clean-up duty in our lives. This lack of acknowledgment and remembrance on our part is nothing more than ingratitude. If we're truly grateful for God's intervention in our lives, we will change the way we function to line up with His desires.

There are many examples in the Bible of people who, when God brought blessings in their lives, allowed their pride to go unchecked, and their blessing became their downfall. King Uzziah in Judah is credited with a lot of success, but he is a prime example of the dangers success can bring. Listed in 2 Chronicles 26 are some of the great accomplishments King Uzziah is known for. He sought the Lord, rebuilt destroyed towns and built new towns, declared war on and defeated the Philistines, built forts and fortified towers, dug wells, and trained warriors. Verse fifteen ends with, *"His fame spread far and wide, for the Lord helped him wonderfully until he became very powerful"* (NLT). Verses sixteen through twenty-one say this,

GOD IS INCREDIBLY GRACIOUS, BUT AT SOME POINT HE WILL EXCUSE HIMSELF FROM CLEAN-UP DUTY IN OUR LIVES.

> *But when he became powerful, he also became proud, which led to his downfall. He sinned against the Lord his God by entering the sanctuary of the Lord's Temple and personally burning incense on the altar. Azariah the high priest went in after him*

with eighty other priests of the Lord, all brave men. They confronted King Uzziah and said, "It is not for you, Uzziah, to burn incense to the Lord. That is the work of the priests alone, the sons of Aaron who are set apart for this work. Get out of the sanctuary, for you have sinned. The Lord God will not honor you for this!" Uzziah was furious and refused to set down the incense burner he was holding. But as he was standing there with the priests before the incense altar in the Lord's temple, leprosy suddenly broke out on his forehead. When Azariah and the other priests saw the leprosy, they rushed him out. And the king himself was eager to get out because the Lord had struck him. So King Uzziah had leprosy until the day he died. He lived in isolation, excluded from the Temple of the Lord... (NLT)

HE ALLOWS DIFFICULTIES AND DELAYS TO COME OUR DIRECTION KNOWING THAT THE FIGHT TO STAY AFLOAT AND MOVE FORWARD IS STRENGTHENING US.

As we work toward and prepare for all God has purposed in our lives, He is focused on refining our character. He allows difficulties and delays to come our direction knowing that the fight to stay afloat and move forward is strengthening us. The success, as it comes, isn't meant to lift us up, but rather to exalt the name of Jesus. Our ability to remain in His shadow holds us steady as we're presented with more visibility. As God opens doors for us, let's press closer into Him. Let the reward of your success be His friendship and His presence.

CHAPTER TEN

Legacy Matters

When I looked up the word legacy in Webster's dictionary, I expected to find a lofty definition, one equal to the weight of the word's connotation. But, all it said was, "A bequest; something to bequeath. A particular thing left by a last will or testament." We can either see this definition as not too impressive, or we can see it as an incredible invitation. The opportunity is wide open—What do I have to give to those around me and to those who come after me?

OUR LIVES BECOME THE BIGGEST MEGAPHONE BY WHICH WE SHOUT HIS FAITHFULNESS.

We all want to live with a feeling of significance. Our lives would be incredibly empty if we didn't believe we have purpose in being alive. Author Dutch Sheets said, "Things are supposed to be different on planet earth because you showed up." Having a desire to leave an imprint or make a lasting impression is part of our DNA, but whether we create an insignificant contribution or a *lasting legacy* with our lives is directly tied to our connection with the Kingdom of God.

As Christians, our highest call is to exalt the name of Jesus. So, our lives become the biggest megaphone by which we shout His faithfulness. Psalm 89:1 (NKJV) exhorts us, *"I will sing of the mercies of the LORD forever; with my mouth will I make known Your faithfulness to all generations."* We must speak of the Lord and His goodness. This verse doesn't say *with my actions,* although actions are important. It doesn't say *with the smile on my face,* although your smile is incredibly important. It says *with my mouth*; we must share our testimonies, recount the faithfulness of God, and speak of the hope within us.

Allow me to speak to each gender for a moment. As women, we have a unique opportunity in creating legacy. We're incredibly relational, which means we tend to have multiple relationships at differing levels of intimacy going on at all times. I have asked God to help me harness this female gift in order to make a Christ-centered impact on an exponentially growing number of people around me. My prayer sounds something like this, "Lord, let Your influence through my life go further than I ever could have imagined." The number one place this influence starts is at home. If you are married and have children, you have two opportunities staring you in the face twenty-four/seven. Yes, you can influence your husband! Does that mean your influence will cause him to be what *you* want him to be? Not necessarily. You don't have authority over your husband. He stands in authority over you, according to the Word of God. So, you are to show respect for his position in the family and BE the picture of Christ. Your influence, over time, will make a huge difference in his life. Pray for him and his success. Although you can't control his actions or his spiritual growth, you can set the atmosphere of Christ in your home.

Men, you have an incredible opportunity to sow seeds of blessing into your wife and children. They need Godly leadership and love that only comes from Him. Your devotional life with the Lord becomes the majority of the legacy you create for your children. Your vocation is secondary to the spiritual relationship. A Godly heritage is the greatest gift you pass down. And, how you treat your wife is not only a testimony to your relationship with the Lord, but also a witness to your children. 1 Peter 3:7 is a sober reminder, *"...You husbands must give honor to your wives. Treat her with understanding as you live together. She may be weaker than you are, but she is your equal partner in God's gift of new life. If you don't treat her as you should, your prayers will not be heard."* That's incredibly clear!

YOUR DEVOTIONAL LIFE WITH THE LORD BECOMES THE MAJORITY OF THE LEGACY YOU CREATE FOR YOUR CHILDREN.

What about our children? This is where it gets really exciting! We have little moldable people in our hands. When my children were born, I thought, "I have eighteen short years to shape, develop, and teach these little ones." I have always viewed them as my greatest masterpiece. Are they perfect? No! Can I control their actions as adults? No! But, I do stand in authority over them while they're growing up. That means I have the ability to pray with all authority over their lives and futures. I can pour into them with every teachable moment I can identify. With three small ones under the age of five, my question became, "How do I raise them to love You,

Lord?" His answer to me was simply, *"Let Me lead you, and they'll follow."* Don't underestimate your responsibility at home. These are your greatest opportunities for maximum impact. Although I've not yet been blessed with grandchildren, I look forward to those years of speaking life into them as I did my own children in their growing up years.

Friends is another category of influence where legacy is birthed—both those who are our hang-out buddies and those who we've gathered around ourselves for the purpose of influence. I take those very seriously with whom God has surrounded me. These are the people I pray for consistently and make time in my schedule to be with. And they pray for me. Be intentional about the time you pour into those who God has brought near (like Jesus did with His disciples). Be available to them. Pray also that God will give you those who are currently going in the direction He has called you. Learn from them.

IT TAKES DELIBERATE EFFORT TO REMEMBER THAT YOUR LIFE IS BEING WATCHED.

Those in your frequent circle, such as a small group, Sunday school class, and coworkers are the next ripple of influence—Although they may not know all your heartfelt victories and defeats, they closely observe your life and are deeply influenced by you. It takes deliberate effort to remember that your life is being watched. So, be careful when choosing words and actions. They influence others more than you realize.

The next group that receives your influence is those who watch your life from afar (crowds, social media). Although you may not ever have a personal relationship with these folks, many of them feel they know you because of your posts. Give them posts that point toward a good attitude and a Christ-centered heart. These are also folks who may be impacted by your speaking, your written work, your creative work, but you may never meet. One afternoon, I went into a copy center to have my book posters printed, and the sales girl and I fell into conversation. She wanted to know what I*n the Stillness* was about, and that was all the introduction I needed! By the time we were finished talking, she had tears in her eyes and was asking a *why question.* (Anytime someone asks a why question, you have an inroad to speak into their lives.) *Why did my loved one have to die? Why did that happen to me?* I ministered to her and told her I would bring her a copy of the book.

YOU ARE A CONDUIT FOR THE MASTER TO MINISTER TO PEOPLE AROUND YOU.

Being aware of your circles of influence is critical because it reminds you that you are not an island. It *does* matter how you live and the choices you make. Your life is not your own. You are a conduit for the Master to minister to people around you.

Now that we've identified who we are influencing, let's talk about five keys to developing and leaving a lasting legacy with our lives. A lasting legacy (one centered on God and His purposes) is first and foremost born out of relationship with God.

As we spend time with God, just knowing His heart, He begins to reveal His dreams for our lives. If you are seeking to know your purpose, pursue Him and His heart, and

He will bring to light what He has designed you for. His dreams for us are tied to the gifts and talents He deposited in us as He formed us, but the intersection of *your gifts* and *His purpose* happens on your knees. Without a God-infusion into your gifts and talents, you may be able to create some great moments for others, but lasting significance will elude you.

Romans 12:2 (NLT) reminds us that knowing God's will for our lives involves allowing Him to change us from the inside out. *"Don't copy the behavior and customs of this world, but let God transform you into a new person by changing the way you think. Then you will know what God wants you to do, and you will know how good and pleasing and perfect his will really is."* Pursue your relationship with the Lord above all else.

Our intimate walk with Jesus begins at the moment of salvation. We recognize and choose Him as our Savior, and we are given the Holy Spirit to help direct our lives. Many people stop there—with salvation—but they are missing the rest of what God intended. They remain as baby Christians, taking instead of giving. As we read His Word, we realize that we need to make Him Lord, not just Savior. This means following His Word in obedience. And, over time, as we learn to love His precepts and pursue His heart, we find that a beautiful friendship with Him has emerged. We have learned to trust Him. It's in this stage of friendship with God that we learn to adventure with Him.

A lasting legacy is not only born out of relationship with God, but it is also carved out by obedience. Learning to keep saying yes to Him is part of our growth as Christians.

God calls those who obey Him His true children. 1 John 3:10 says, *"So now we can tell who are children of God and who are children of the Devil. Anyone who does not obey God's commands and does not love other Christians does not belong to God."*

So, lasting legacy is not only born out of relationship with God and carved out by obedience, it is also maintained by gratitude. Remember that anything good in your life is because of the Father. This constant reminder helps us maintain an attitude of gratitude even in the midst of life's many challenges.

A lasting legacy is also carried out through service to others. Our biggest obstacle to living out the life God has for us is us. Any time we become too focused on ourselves, we settle. We settle for the monotony of life. We settle for earthbound dreaming instead of God-sized dreaming. God wants to continually stretch us because that causes us to rely on Him, and His heart is always focused on others. Part of what we can do to stay focused on others is to create margin in our lives. Leave extra time in going from place to place to notice people. Speak to individuals as they cross your path. It's so easy for us to be in such a hurry that we don't smile at those we pass or stop for a minute to talk. Ask God to order your steps each day and expect to encounter people who would benefit from a few minutes of your attention.

ANY TIME WE BECOME TOO FOCUSED ON OURSELVES, WE SETTLE.

Finally, a lasting legacy is bathed in prayer. Love is our greatest offensive weapon to the people around us, both to those who are easy to love and those who spitefully use us. God doesn't differentiate between these two groups when we're commanded to love. So, pray for both categories of people. Ephesians 3:14-19 is a beautiful prayer pattern we can pray over the people who directly affect our lives. Just fill in the blanks with the person's name for whom you are praying.

> *For this cause I bow my knees unto the Father of our Lord Jesus Christ, of whom the whole family in heaven and earth is named, that he would grant _______, according to the riches of his glory, to be strengthened with might by his Spirit in _______'s inner man; that Christ may dwell in _______'s heart by faith; that _______, being rooted and grounded in love, may be able to comprehend with all saints what is the breadth, and length, and depth, and height; and to know the love of Christ, which passeth knowledge, that _______ might be filled with all the fullness of God." (KJV)*

LOVE IS OUR GREATEST OFFENSIVE WEAPON TO THE PEOPLE AROUND US.

As we consider the lasting legacy we have the privilege of creating with our lives, two cautions arise. Both fear and pride will negate legacy. Let's address fear first. Legacy isn't created by walking in safety. It requires stepping out. And, stepping out in faith is risky. I'm reminded of a quote by Dr. Lilian B. Yeomans that hung on my refrigerator all of my children's growing up years. "God delights in His children stepping out over the aching void with nothing underneath their feet but the Word of God." As we learn to rely on God and all of His goodness, fear gives way to His love, and we're able to proceed in trust.

We touched on pride in earlier chapters as we discussed position, influence, and success. It's influence that *creates* legacy. There's nothing wrong with position, but position itself doesn't create a lasting legacy. Pride relies on position. Humility relies on God's anointing. You can still be in position, but have lost His anointing. And, conversely, you can have God's anointing, but not have a position. I would rather walk in His anointing, creating influence with my life than to walk in position (without His anointing) and lose my influence due to pride. Position is an opportunity for even greater influence if we keep our pride in check.

> BOTH FEAR AND PRIDE WILL NEGATE LEGACY.

Legacy is ultimately about developing a lifestyle of faithfulness, commitment, obedience, and finishing well. Legacy is you taking up the baton and running your lap faithfully, creating a seamless proclamation of His faithfulness from the generations that came before you to the generations yet to come. He lives in you today—now carry forward the proclamation of the name of Jesus!

As a final thought, we have a responsibility beyond our families and our individual lives. We are part of God's Kingdom army, which means we have a cause to advance. This nation is in a dire state, and it's up to us, as believers, to see ourselves as responsible for the condition of our nation. 2 Chronicles 7:14 says, *"Then if my people who are called by my name will humble themselves and pray and seek my face and turn from their wicked ways, I will hear from Heaven, and will forgive their sin and restore their land."* (NLT) Our greatest contribution to legacy comes in prayer. May we be faithful to spend time on our knees praying Heaven down to Earth.

Other Books by Deborah Rae Stricklin

The Journey

Dreaming God-sized is not for the faint-hearted. Courage, faith, self-control, wisdom, humility, and unprecedented patience are all required as God unleashes the process of dream fulfillment in our lives. We tend to focus on the end result of the dream, while God focuses on the transforming process in us. We stretch. We grow. We become. Through adversity, resistance, and painful circumstances, God refines us until we are finally ready to give birth to His dream. Then, and only then, will the fulfillment of the dream yield its true harvest – the exaltation of the name of Jesus Christ.

Come to the Mountain

The Scriptural term "mountain of God" traditionally refers to locations, such as Mount Sinai, which represent a place where people sought refuge in God's presence. The beauty of rest and peace in Him can be found as He draws us into His presence, just as He beckoned biblical heroes of old. His purpose in drawing us to Himself is always to knit our hearts with His. If we'll have the courage to respond when He calls, our lives will be forever changed.

The Tempted

We, as humans, are The Tempted. When we allow distance to exist between us and our loving Creator, we position ourselves to give into what tempts us. The power that falsely binds us to sin is unmasked as we confront the lies that have separated us from the love of our heavenly Father. That which tempts us loses its power as we stand strong in the grip of His love. This book is about us, the tempted, and our human response to separation from our Heavenly Father. It's about understanding what causes us to yield to sin when we should be standing strong. That's a topic we all need!

Sacrifice Required

The Kingdom of God is founded on the coming of Jesus Christ, our permanent sacrifice and perfect example. As devoted members of His Kingdom, sacrifice is our Christian heritage as well as our challenge to grow in Christ-likeness. For us, then, what does a sacrificial life look like? It begins, most notably, with living from an eternal perspective – a life lived with Heaven and others in mind. Just as Jesus encountered the weight of the cross, we all face pivotal moments when we must choose between self and sacrifice. And, forward movement in the Kingdom of God rests on our response.

In the Stillness

These difficult circumstances can actually lead us into moments of quiet, resolved hope. The stillness that follows our initial pain in the midst of our loss is critical; this is where faith shines most brightly. In the stillness comes the complete and utter assurance that the hard work of faith is finished, and the rest is left to God. This is not the end of your story, but rather the beginning of a bright, new day. Keep living. Keep moving forward. The One who cannot fail us goes before us.

CPSIA information can be obtained
at www.ICGtesting.com
Printed in the USA
LVOW12s0402261116
514372LV00001B/2/P

9 781943 294459